THE ANCIENT MONUMENTS OF ORKNEY

Anna Ritchie
and
Graham Ritchie

Series editor
David J Breeze, BA, PhD, FSA, FSA Scot
Inspector of Ancient Monuments

D1471462

Historic Buildings and Monuments
Scottish Development Department

Edinburgh
Her Majesty's Stationery Office

The plans of the monuments have been re-drawn, and in some cases simplified, from the published sources. Monuments of similar type have been drawn to consistent scales to permit comparison, and the writers are greatly indebted to Mr S Scott for his skill in preparing and drawing the plans. The drawings of pottery and small finds are the work of Miss A S Henshall, and we are grateful for her permission to use these illustrations in this volume. The map has been drawn by Mr D R Boyd. We are also grateful to those friends and colleagues who have commented on various sections of the guidebook; the views expressed in the final form are, however, the responsibility of the authors alone.

Contents

Brough of Birsay from the air.

'A HERITAGE OF ISLANDS'

The Physical Background

UNTIL the exploits of the Vikings drew attention to northern lands, the Orkneys were virtually on the edge of the known world. They lay far from the centres of innovation and technological progress throughout the prehistoric and early historic periods, but their inhabitants were rarely slow to develop new skills or to adopt new ideas. The fact that so many exceptional monuments survive in the Orkneys is no mere accident of preservation. It is true that the land has not suffered from the high degree of destruction caused by urban and industrial development or by deep ploughing and forestry as have other areas of Scotland; the main threat here is marine erosion. But what is remarkable about the Orkneys is not simply that a great number of monuments has survived, but that so many of them are in themselves outstanding human achievements.

There are almost seventy islands in the Orkney archipelago, mostly formed by rocks of the Middle Old Red Sandstone apart from the hills of Hoy which consist of Upper Old Red Sandstone rocks. There are thus plenty of good sandstones and flagstones for building purposes and, because they split easily along clear bedding planes, they present little difficulty in quarrying. It was this abundance of good stone that led to the development of a tradition of fine dry-stone building early in the prehistoric settlement of the Orkneys. The landscape is typical of that produced by Old Red Sandstone, predominantly gentle and rounded, but rising to spectacularly sculpted cliffs along the west and north coasts.

As an area for primary settlement the Orkneys would have appeared very attractive to early man. Although not quite as bare of trees as today, the islands were unencumbered by the dense forest-cover which made so much of mainland Scotland difficult for early farmers to clear. Light woodlands of alder, birch and willow grew in hollows where there was some shelter from the wind; otherwise the land was open and ready for mixed farming.

Prehistoric Monuments

The ancient monuments of the Orkneys may be appreciated in a number of different ways—the romantic visitor may envisage them as sculpture in a rolling landscape, the historically-minded will try to people the castles and churches with warriors and priests, and the prehistorian, perhaps the most prosaic visitor, will see the tombs, the brochs and the artefacts found in them as a means of reconstructing the life of earlier societies. The range of such prehistoric monuments in Orkney is full and exciting, with the houses and tombs of the earliest agricultural inhabitants, barrows of the second millennium BC, and brochs of the period around the birth of Christ. Recent excavations have, with the aid of radiocarbon dates, provided a longer chronological framework for the Orkney monuments than was previously thought likely, and the dates outlined in this introduction are based on such radiocarbon determinations and take into account the appropriate adjustments that have to be made. This dating method is based on the measurement of the minute quantity of

5

radio-active carbon that is present in all living things (such as trees or animals), but which decays slowly after death. By assuming that the rate of decay is constant, it is possible to determine how long ago an animal died by measuring the remaining radio-activity in an animal bone. There are now radiocarbon dates for a number of sites in Orkney, and some of the earliest dates indicate that small communities began to settle in Orkney by the middle of the fourth millennium BC. They brought with them the cattle and sheep that formed their stock and the grain for their first harvests. The skills of stock-rearing and agriculture are of European and ultimately Near Eastern origin, but the first Orcadians were probably related to neolithic communities on the Atlantic seaways of western Scotland and also on the eastern coast of Britain, rather than immigrants direct from the continent.

Settlements

The way of life of these farming peoples may be reconstructed from two types of evidence, firstly their houses and their burial places (of the latter no less than eleven are in state care) and secondly the material recovered from archaeological excavation—pottery, flint and animal bones. Very few settlement sites of this period are known from Britain, and Orkney is fortunate to possess four of them, three in state care, Knap of Howar, Skara Brae and Links of Noltland on Westray (the last is not open to the public); there is nothing to be seen at the fourth site, Rinyo on the island of Rousay. The houses of the neolithic inhabitants of the islands were of fine dry-stone masonry and, because of the comparative absence of timber and the

These two houses at Knap of Howar on Papa Westray are probably the oldest standing houses in north-west Europe.

availability of good stone, even the internal fittings of the houses at Skara Brae (dressers, beds, and boxes) were carefully built of slabs. Excavation has shown that the earliest houses in Orkney, and indeed probably among the earliest standing houses in north-west Europe, are those known as Knap of Howar on Papa Westray. Here two well-built houses, first excavated in the 1930s, have been shown by a series of radiocarbon dates to have been built about the middle of the fourth millennium. House 1 was divided into two by a partition of slabs and timber posts, and wood must also have played a part in roofing the house. The inhabitants reared cattle, sheep and pigs, and there is evidence to show that they also grew grain. But they did not scorn the natural resources of the island; hunting is indicated by deer bones, and the importance of shell-fish in the diet is demonstrated by oysters, limpets, scallops, whelks and razor-shells. Quantities of sherds of pottery were found in the course of the excavation and, although none of the vessels is complete, the pottery style is quite distinctive and belongs to a class which has been discovered in the chambered tombs of Orkney and is known as Unstan ware. This fact is of considerable importance as, until the identification of Knap of Howar as a neolithic settlement, we knew nothing of the habitation sites of the builders of the most numerous class of chambered tombs; we now have one site of this period as well as an indication of the date of the Unstan ware style of pottery as a whole.

House 1 at Skara Brae. In the centre is the hearth, with the entrance to a cell top left, bed top centre and dresser to the right.

Skara Brae provides one of the most vivid insights into the life of prehistoric man. The final phase of the village, as we see it today, is the result of several reorganisations and reconstructions and, when V G Childe excavated the site in the 1920s, he found deep midden deposits, representing the debris of everyday life over a considerable period. Childe's excavations were designed to discover and conserve the buildings of the settlement; more recent work has been undertaken to provide environmental and dating evidence for the site. Two types of house may be distinguished; the earlier (for example House 9), built round a central hearth, comprises two beds built into the thickness of the wall and a circular cell set into one corner of the wall. The later type (House 7 for example) is considerably larger and brings the beds into the main living area with small cupboards in the wall behind them. In the centre of the houses there were square kerbed hearths with the remains of fires. The beds on either side of the hearth would have been made comfortable with animal skins and heather. The purpose of the dresser is clear, less so the deep slab-boxes set into the floor, the corners of which were carefully sealed with clay in order to hold liquid, perhaps to soak limpets for fish-bait. The inhabitants were settled farmers, as animal bones (cattle, sheep) and grains of cultivated cereal prove, but they were also fishermen and at least occasionally hunters as well. Artefacts comparable to those discovered at Skara Brae have been found on two other types of site—in the chambered tomb at Quoyness on the island of Sanday and at the henge monument and stone circle of the Stones of Stenness—and we shall see that in broad terms at least such monuments may be contemporary. The pottery found at Skara Brae and the Stones of Stenness belongs to the grooved ware type. Such vessels are of a coarse, gritty fabric decorated with incisions, applied bands and plastic ornament. In contrast to the round-based bowls of Unstan ware, grooved ware pots have flat bases and we can imagine such pots

sitting firmly on the dressers at Skara Brae. Grooved ware is found in south and east England and has a scattered distribution in Scotland; radiocarbon dates show that such pottery was in use between the middle of the third millennium and the beginning of the second millennium BC.

Chambered Tombs
Burial and ritual monuments of the fourth and third millennia BC are well represented in the Orkneys. Chambered tombs were burial-vaults built to receive interments over a long period, and they may well have been the focus for other forms of ritual or worship which the techniques of archaeology cannot detect. Excavation of the burial-chambers of such tombs has been undertaken with increasingly scientific methods since the middle of the nineteenth century, most notably by G Petrie and J Farrer in the last century, by W G Grant and J G Callander in the 1930s and by V G Childe in the 1950s. Miss A S Henshall has identified two main classes of tomb, the first known as the Orkney-Cromarty group and the second called after the tomb of Maes Howe. The former group is widepread in north and west Scotland, and the Orcadian stalled cairns and the tombs of the Bookan type are local architectural variants.

The Orcadian stalled cairns are characterised by rectangular chambers set within either circular or roughly rectangular cairns—the chambers are subdivided by pairs of upright slabs into individual compartments or burial-lairs. The Orkney examples are a local adaptation of a basic type of tomb, consisting of entrance-passage and burial-chamber, found in several areas of Atlantic Europe—the passage grave. Not surprisingly the Orkney tombs are closely related to those of Caithness and Sutherland, and Knowe of Yarso for instance may be thought of as a developed version of tombs in Caithness. The elaboration and lengthening of the chamber, as at Midhowe, may represent a still later stage. At both Knowe of Yarso and Midhowe the passage and chamber are on the same axis, but at another group of sites (Blackhammer and Unstan) the passage is at right angles to the chamber. This may be a parallel or indeed a later development of the basic plan. These tombs, Taversoe Tuick included, give the impression of being unified architectural concepts, and there is nothing to suggest that they were subject to reconstruction or alteration during their use, though such evidence is increasingly being found on other sites. Even the extraordinary cairn of Taversoe Tuick, where the two chambers are superimposed one above the other, seems to be the result of a deliberate plan, although it

The interior of Unstan chambered tomb; the entrance to the side cell is to the left.

may well have been built in stages. One of the few Orkney tombs to show traces of multi-period construction is on the small island of Calf Eday (not in state care).

The discovery of skeletal remains, pottery and flint is more difficult to interpret as it is currently thought likely that the chambers were used to receive burials over a long period and that the chambers or sections of them may have been cleared out in order to make room for further burials. It follows, therefore, that what is recovered in the course of an excavation are the burial deposits of the final phase before the tomb was sealed permanently or went out of use— perhaps with the extinction of a family line. Some earlier deposits may have been put to one side, but they would be difficult to

9

disentangle. The tombs of the Orkney-Cromarty series that are in state care (Unstan, Blackhammer, Knowe of Yarso, Midhowe and Taversoe Tuick) have produced both skeletal material and deposits of pottery. Most information comes from Midhowe where twenty-five individuals were found; where still intact they were crouched burials, but in other cases the bones had been gathered together to form a heap in the centre of the compartment. At Knowe of Yarso, where there were the remains of twenty-nine interments, earlier burials had been neatly re-arranged, with several groups of skulls placed in rows. It is possible that the cremations found in cists at Taversoe Tuick belong to a late stage in the use of the chamber. Isbister on South Ronaldsay is open to the public, although not in state care, and excavations there have added considerably to our understanding of

The interior of Maes Howe showing the entrance to one of the burial chambers.

chambered tombs. Not only was there a marked concentration of skulls in one of the side-cells, but the carcases of sea-eagles had been placed deliberately in the chamber, hinting perhaps at totemic ideas. The twenty-four dog skulls in Cuween may also represent a tribal emblem.

The pottery deposited with the burials is rarely associated with a particular interment. At Midhowe, for example, pottery lay in a little heap on the opposite side of the chamber from the burials. The most important pottery assemblage is that from Unstan, where the bulk of it was recovered from a single compartment. The major deposit may possibly have been associated with several crouched skeletons, and this might be interpreted as the final deposit in the chamber, but the excavation report cannot be precisely interpreted. What is clear, however, is that the style of pottery known as Unstan ware, dated to the mid-fourth millennium BC at Knap of Howar and extending in date into the third millennium

BC, provides a broad chronological horizon for these chambered tombs. Apart from Unstan itself, Unstan ware has been found at Blackhammer, Midhowe and Taversoe Tuick. One sherd from Unstan has the impression of a grain of barley—an indication of the agricultural activities of the community.

A sub-group of the Orkney-Cromarty tombs, sometimes known as the Bookan type, is characterised by oval or rectangular chambers subdivided into compartments by upright slabs projecting radially from the side walls. The lower chamber and the miniature chamber of Taversoe Tuick are examples of this type and both have involved cutting into the rock in order to hollow out the space for the chamber. Such engineering expertise would also have been essential for the careful cutting of the chamber and passage for the other example of this group— the Dwarfie Stane on the island of Hoy. This rock-cut tomb in its bleak setting is a monument most evocative of the religious fervour of the early inhabitants of Orkney.

The chambered tombs of the second series are named after the magnificent tomb of Maes Howe. Of the ten or eleven examples of this type, no less than five are in state care: Maes Howe, Cuween Hill, Wideford Hill, Quoyness and Holm of Papa Westray. At Maes Howe itself, a central chamber is entered by a long passage leading in from the edge of the mound, and there is a small cell opening off each of the other three walls of the chamber. The overall plan of the tomb thus resembles a cross. The tombs on Cuween Hill and Wideford Hill are very similar to Maes Howe, but at Quoyness and Holm of Papa Westray the basic plan has been elaborated by the addition of more cells, and this has resulted in the elongation of the central chamber. The problems of interpretation of the burials and grave-goods are identical to those of the Orkney-Cromarty class. Burials were found at Cuween Hill and Quoyness but do not appear to have survived at the other sites. Only at Quoyness have any accompanying grave-goods been recovered—pottery, spiked stone objects and a large bone pin with a knob on one side. The stone objects (which have been interpreted as ceremonial maceheads) and the bone pin belong to types that can be paralleled at Skara Brae.

Prior to the development of radiocarbon dating, the architectural sophistication of Maes Howe seemed to indicate that this tomb was the earliest of the group. A C Renfrew's excavation of the Maes Howe type of tomb at Quanterness (not in state care) in 1972-4, and concurrent work at Maes Howe itself, together with a series of dates from these sites and from Quoyness, now suggest an alternative hypothesis. Maes Howe is seen not at the beginning of the series but as the result of an existing local building tradition represented by Quanterness and Quoyness.

Stone Circles

The survival of settlement sites is very much a matter of chance, and we are fortunate to have Knap of Howar and Skara Brae; the stone mounds of chambered tombs have a higher chance of survival and, except in those cases where they have been completely removed for agricultural reasons, it is likely that a comparatively complete distribution remains. Childe has suggested that the tombs on Rousay are grouped in a way that corresponds to the main concentrations of modern population, and that each tomb may have represented a unit of farmland settled by a group of households. The converse is true in the case of the stone circles and henge monuments of Orkney, for here we may be dealing not with a family or local unit but with a much larger social unit; these monuments form a great ceremonial centre, the focus for religious or legal ritual for the islands as a whole. Henge monuments are a peculiarly British phenomenon and are usually earthwork circles comprising an inner ditch and outer bank with either one or two entrance causeways across the ditch and through the bank. A small proportion of such sites contain stone circles within the

The Stenness area looking west, Maes Howe lies in the foreground with the Stones of Stenness behind. In the background is the Ring of Brodgar.

enclosed areas; at the Stones of Stenness and the Ring of Brodgar the ditches have surrounded impressive circles of standing stones. The Stones of Stenness, which is likely to be the earlier site and probably dates to the early third millennium BC, originally comprised a circle of twelve stones set within a rock-cut ditch and outer bank. The single entrance-causeway means that the site belongs to the earlier group of henge monuments, while the Ring of Brodgar with two entrances belongs to the later. The erection of the standing stones and the quarrying of the ditch would clearly have been undertaken over a long period. The use of the site is, however, broadly contemporary with Skara Brae and the Maes Howe type of tombs such as Quoyness. Sherds of grooved ware were discovered in the central stone setting and also at the bottom of the ditch, along with animal bones which might suggest feasting or sacrifice.

There is every reason to believe that the building of such a site, involving the quarrying from the ditch of many tonnes of stone, would be a long and probably seasonal undertaking. The engineering feat of the building of the Ring of Brodgar is even greater—a larger amount of stone was removed and the sixty standing stones positioned on an uneven site with a very high degree of accuracy. No excavation has been carried out within the Ring and our information about the nearby barrows is equally slight.

Barrows and Standing Stones
The chronology of the second millennium BC over much of Britain is based on a consideration of pottery styles and bronze finds from burial deposits and chance discoveries. In Orkney, however, recognisable pottery is rare, and, for the most part, beakers, food vessels, cinerary urns and bronze finds are absent; for the period between about 2000 BC and about 1000 BC there are thus few fixed points and it is

difficult to correlate the various types of evidence. Only a small number of monuments of this period are in state care— the barrows, or earthen burial-mounds, at Brodgar and some of the isolated standing stones. Recent excavations have suggested that the 'burnt mounds' of Orkney, the remnants of cooking places sometimes with adjacent houses, may also be of Bronze Age date. A new burial ritual was introduced after 2000 BC involving individual interment in a small stone coffin or cist, which was set into an earthen mound or cairn. Cists are often now found as a result of ploughing. They may contain inhumation or cremation burials, in some cases accompanied by grave-goods such as a steatite cinerary urn or a stone pot-lid. It is possible that chambered tombs continued to be used to receive burials into the Bronze Age. At Knowe of Yarso, for example, sherds of a food vessel were discovered at a rather higher level than most of the other objects in the inner half of the inner compartment. The cremation deposits in the upper chamber at Taversoe Tuick and the burials in the filling of Midhowe may all be secondary deposits in a building known to be sacred.

Brochs

For southern and eastern Scotland, history began with the recorded military campaign of Agricola and the Roman army in AD 80, but the Orkneys remained in the strict sense prehistoric until well into the middle centuries of the first millennium when they came into the ambit of the Celtic Church. There is no Roman period in the far north of Scotland, and the closest that any Roman came to the Orkneys, as we learn from the classical writer Tacitus, was when Agricola's fleet sailed round the north and established the fact that Britain was an island. It is likely that Tacitus exaggerates when he claims that Agricola discovered the Orkneys and subdued them. Roman coins and sherds of pottery have been found in the Orkneys, but these represent nothing more than booty from raiding expeditions or the gains of trade

with areas further south.

From the last few centuries BC, Orkney was again the scene of flourishing building activities. This was the era of broch-building, when great stone towers or brochs were constructed throughout northern Scotland and the western and northern islands. Although details of their architecture may vary, in basic plan brochs are a uniform and highly impressive class of monument; they are circular dry-stone towers, from 11 m to 15 m in overall diameter at the base, and they were built with such thick walls (3.7 m to 4.6 m) that they could rise to considerable heights. The tallest surviving broch-tower is that on the island of Mousa in Shetland, which is still about 13 m high and was originally even taller, and there the walls occupy 64 per cent of the total diameter. For stability the diameter of the tower decreases as it rises and the effect is a profile very similar to that of a modern cooling-tower. A single entrance at ground level was the only opening in the smooth outer face of the broch, but inside there were openings into cells, stairways and galleries built within the thickness of the tower-wall. A ledge or scarcement running horizontally round the inner face of the tower at a height of 2 m or 3 m above the floor supported a timber gallery, and the roof, evidence for which rarely survives, must also have been timber-framed.

Brochs were highly defensible structures in themselves but sometimes they were strengthened even further by encircling ramparts and ditches; such outlying defences are particularly well illustrated by two brochs in state care, Gurness and Midhowe. Three lines of rampart and ditch protect Gurness broch, while at Midhowe a single massive rampart was built, sandwiched between a pair of ditches. In some cases, it is possible that the earthwork defences represent an earlier fort to which a broch was added, rather than defences contemporary with the broch.

Defence was clearly a major factor in the design of brochs, but it is difficult to identify

13

the underlying reason that made such defensive measures necessary. Iron Age society seems to have been turbulent and aggressive everywhere—forts were built on the mainland of Scotland throughout the middle and later first millennium BC, the period of the Iron Age—but, in the absence of written sources, we cannot discover either by whom or against whom the brochs were built in any particular area. Like medieval castles, brochs were permanently occupied family homes rather than occasional retreats; their internal fittings include hearths, storage tanks and often a water-supply in the form of a natural spring, and a wide range of domestic equipment has been found in them in the course of excavation. The plans of brochs and castles are here drawn to the same scale, and it can be seen that they are indeed comparable structures, the fortified residences of the upper classes in similarly stratified societies.

The Broch of Gurness from the air. The broch and its surrounding settlement is protected by a series of ramparts and ditches. A later group of houses, discovered during excavations to lie on top of earlier building to one side of the broch, was dismantled and rebuilt on the right. (Reproduced by kind permission of the Royal Commission on the Ancient and Historical Monuments of Scotland)

There are currently two theories as to how and where the idea of building brochs developed. One theory takes the high concentration of brochs in the Orkneys as proof that they originated there in response to local conditions, their design aided by the availability of excellent building-stone and by an existing tradition of building large stone-walled round houses from which the idea of building taller versions could have been developed. The other school of thought argues that the earliest brochs must be those most similar in lay-out to the earlier stone forts from which they evolved; since the closest similarities between brochs and forts are found in the Hebrides, the idea of building brochs is thus seen to have spread northwards and eastwards from a Hebridean source. Only more excavation leading to a detailed understanding of the relative dates of brochs throughout Scotland will solve the question of their origin.

The settlements that grew up around the brochs look very cluttered and crowded in the form in which they survive today, particularly at Gurness, but this is the result of several centuries of building and rebuilding and alterations to old houses. At Gurness, there would seem initially to have been a row of semi-detached houses partially encircling the broch-tower. These were essentially sub-rectangular buildings with good dry-stone walls and carefully kerbed hearths, but they were divided into rooms and alcoves by upright slabs and minor walls which proliferated over the years. Whatever the social conditions that demanded the building of fortified towers, by the late second century AD conditions seem to have altered and brochs were gradually being modified, abandoned or even dismantled. This change in status is clearly seen at Gurness and Midhowe, where the broch-towers were used as sources of stone to build new structures both inside and outside the now abandoned brochs, and where the original outlying defences were slighted and built over.

Outside the broch at Gurness is a village. This view shows a group of houses beside the main street to the left.

Earth-houses

It is possible that some at least of the Orcadian earth-houses belong to this period after the abandonment of brochs, but others may date to the later first millennium BC, on analogy with evidence from Jarlshof in Shetland. The date and function of earth-houses are outstanding problems in the archaeology of the Orkneys and they will be solved only by excavation.

Picts and Norsemen

The people living in settlements such as those at Gurness and Midhowe were the descendants of the broch-builders, and they form a bridge, in archaeological terms, between prehistory and history. By the fourth century AD, the name *Picti* had begun to appear in the works of classical authors concerned with northern Britain, and it is certain that, by the sixth century at least and probably earlier, the Orkneys were part of the Pictish kingdom. Adomnan, the biographer of St Columba, records that there were Orcadians at the court of the Pictish king Bridei during Columba's visit around

Three warriors march across this Pictish symbol stone found at the Brough of Birsay. The original stone is now in the Royal Museum of Scotland, Queen Street, Edinburgh, but a copy has been erected on the site.

565; the Orcadians are described as hostages in a way that suggests that, although they had their own local ruler, the Orkneys recognised Bridei as their overlord.

The most distinctively Pictish objects found in the Orkneys are the decorated stone slabs known as Pictish symbol stones. None survives as a standing monument, but a cast of the slab found in the Early Christian cemetery on the Brough of Birsay has been erected on the site and gives a good impression of the original appearance of such stones. The repertoire of Pictish art included abstract symbols, fantasy animals and realistic designs of animals and human figures, and the standard of craftsmanship was often very high. The purpose of the symbol stones is obscure; only very rarely have they been found in an archaeological context that gives any clue to their function, and even then the context is secondary in the sense that the stone has obviously been re-used. It is possible that the stones did not all serve the same purpose; about 250 stones have been found, distributed over the whole of Pictland from Shetland to the Firth of Forth and dating from the centuries between about AD 600 and 900, and some variety of function would not be surprising. Among the explanations that have been put forward in recent years are that they were tombstones, personal memorial monuments, landmarkers showing territorial boundaries, or public monuments commemorating important marriage alliances between great families. Some stones bear inscriptions carved in the ogam alphabet but these are unfortunately unintelligible; the Picts are believed to have spoken two languages, one Celtic and one an unknown non-Indo-European tongue, and the ogam inscriptions would appear to have been written in the latter.

Both symbols and ogam letters have been found carved on small personal objects as well as the stone slabs. A bone knife-handle bearing ogam letters was recovered at Gurness, and an inscribed spindle-whorl was found during excavations on the Point of

16

Buckquoy at Birsay. This site, now destroyed, was a Pictish family farmstead and included two houses very similar in plan to the late five-celled house at Gurness. It was occupied in the seventh and eighth centuries and may have been connected in some way, perhaps as the home farm, with the Early Christian settlement on the Brough of Birsay.

The Brough of Birsay is a site of exceptional interest and importance, for its known settlement spanned not just the Early Christian period but the Norse period as well and continued into medieval times. The buildings and cemetery of the early ecclesiastical site were overlain by a fine Norse church with its own graveyard and associated buildings. The nature of the Norse settlement was certainly not wholly or even primarily ecclesiastical, and the hall-houses so typical of the early Viking Age are here preserved in a condition matched only at Jarlshof in Shetland.

The Orkneys were first settled by Norsemen around AD 800 and they soon became a nodal point on the western seaways. The Norse earldom of the Orkneys, Shetland and Caithness grew into a powerful political unit, and the events recorded in *Orkneyinga Saga* make exciting reading. The Saga was written about AD 1200 by an author whose name and parentage are unknown, but who is thought to have lived in, or at least to have known best, the area around Thurso on the north coast of Caithness. Much of the early part of the Saga is fictitious, but there is

The Maes Howe dragon carved by Norsemen in the twelfth century AD.

The surviving fragment of the round church at Orphir: this is a view of the apse.

17

a strong element of reliable history in the later chapters. The Saga ends with the terrible burning of Bishop Adam at Halkirk in Caithness, a deed which led to the murder of Earl John in the cellar of a Thurso inn in 1231 and thereby ended the Norse line of earls.

There is a growing body of evidence, both from excavations and from a re-appraisal of ninth- and tenth-century sculpture, to show that the incoming Norse settlers of the ninth century adopted many ideas and traditions from the indigenous Picts. Once the Norse settlement was firmly established, the Pictish element lost its separate identity and the cultural life of the Orkneys became entirely that of a Norse earldom. It was certainly no parochial colony and the far-ranging interests and activities of Viking-Age Orcadians are well attested by the surviving monuments of the late eleventh and twelfth centuries—by the round church at Orphir with its links with Jerusalem and the Crusades, and, above all, by the superb Cathedral of St Magnus in Kirkwall.

Later Monuments

After the murder of the last of the Norse earls of Orkney in 1231, the title passed to the son of the Earl of Angus, a Scotsman who in respect of his title owed allegiance to the Norwegian Crown. Following the Battle of Largs in 1263 and the loss of the Western Isles to the Scottish Crown as a result of the Treaty of Perth in 1266, only the Northern Isles remained Norse possessions. The increasing control of Orkney by earls who were of Scottish origin, culminating in the appointment of Henry Sinclair, Earl of Roslin, to the earldom in 1379, led to changes in the ownership of land and the break-up of Norse systems of tenure. The Northern Isles were officially held by the Sinclairs of the Norwegian and later of the Danish Crown until their annexation to the Scottish Crown as a result of the dowry agreement made on the marriage of James III of Scotland with Margaret, the daughter of King Christian I of Norway and Denmark in 1468. By this agreement Orkney was held as a pledge,

redeemable by the payment of 50,000 Rhenish florins, with the residue of the dowry, 10,000 florins, to be paid in cash. The following year it remained unpaid and Shetland was therefore pledged for 8,000 florins. Two years later, as the pledges had not been redeemed, the earldom of Orkney and the Lordship of Shetland were annexed to the Scottish Crown. In the following century Norse systems of landholding and government steadily gave way to Scottish customs, and indeed Scottish landowners, and by the late seventeenth century the Norse language was spoken by the inhabitants of only two or three parishes.

In 1564 Queen Mary made a grant of the royal estates in Orkney and Shetland to Robert Stewart, her half-brother, and a natural son of James V. His tenure of office has been concisely narrated: 'This miscreant, having secured in addition the whole temporal estates of the bishopric by an excambion (exchange) effected in 1568, and having become Earl of Orkney in 1581, spent the rest of his life—with the exception of a short period during which he was imprisoned, partly as a penalty for improper negotiations with Denmark—in oppressing the islanders for his own personal advantage.' The architectural legacy of Earl Robert and his son Patrick (1592-1615) is, however, of outstanding interest. The Palace at Birsay, built for Earl Robert in 1574, is a courtyard building overlooking the sheltered bay at the most northern part of mainland. The surviving walls give little impression of the formerly rich internal decoration of the building. Earl Patrick was even more ambitious, and his palace at Kirkwall, begun in 1606, is spacious and well-proportioned. In contrast, Noltland Castle on the island of Westray is a grim military building dating to between 1560 and 1573 and is notable as an example of a Z-plan castle; the lavish provision of gun-loops betrays the ruthlessness of Gilbert Balfour for whom it was built.

Two nineteenth-century monuments are in state care—the Martello Tower at

Hackness and the horizontal water-mill or click mill at Dounby. The twin Martello Towers guarding the Longhope anchorage are a reminder of the importance of Orkney on Britain's trade route to Northern Europe in the early nineteenth century. Only three Martello Towers were built in Scotland, two in Orkney and one at Leith on the Forth, and it is appropriate that the tower at Hackness should be restored as an example of the military architecture of this period. Click Mill, Dounby, is an attractive example of a horizontal water-mill, a type once common in Orkney and Shetland.

Earl's Palace, Kirkwall.

Ring of Brodgar: pen and ink wash by R Pococke, 1760.
(Reproduced by kind permission of the British Library)

'STUPENDOUS MONUMENTS OF ANTIQUITY'

Scattered over the mainland of Orkney and the islands is a remarkable range of well-preserved monuments illustrating every major phase of building achievement over past centuries; the examples now in the care of Historic Buildings and Monuments reflect many aspects of Orcadian history, from the wartime importance of Scapa Flow anchorages in the 19th and 20th centuries, underlined by the Martello Towers of Hoy, to the once familiar water-mills essential to the daily bread of a farming people. The political turbulence and wealth of medieval times is graphically portrayed by the grim castle of Noltland and the splendour of the Earls' Palaces of Birsay and Kirkwall. Spiritual and communal life is represented over a long period from an unusual variety of early medieval churches to the great stone circles of remote prehistory, and Orkney is particularly fortunate in the number and quality of early stone-built tombs open to the public. All too often, it is the everyday, domestic aspects of the past that remain obscure, but here the abundance of good building stone has ensured the survival not just of the state monuments of great men but also of the homes of ordinary people: the hall-houses of Norse settlers on the Brough of Birsay, the massed housing of iron-age villagers round the chieftain's broch at Gurness, the dwellings and work-shops of neolithic farmers at Skara Brae and Knap of Howar.

The monuments described in detail below are arranged in chronological order, beginning with the tombs and settlements of the 4th and 3rd millennia. The chambered tombs (1-11) are treated in the two groups outlined in the Introduction: first the Orkney-Cromarty tombs, beginning with Unstan on Mainland and then the tombs on the island of Rousay (Blackhammer, Knowe of Yarso, Midhowe and Taversoe Tuick), and second the Maes Howe group, with Maes Howe, Cuween Hill and Wideford Hill on Mainland, Quoyness on Sanday and the cairn on Holm of Papa Westray; finally there is a description of the Dwarfie Stane on Hoy. Some of the chambers and side-cells are dark, and visitors will find a torch useful.

21

1 Unstan Chambered Tomb, Mainland

Although the chambered tomb of Unstan lacks its original roof, the restored outward impression of an upturned pudding-bowl gives a good idea of the original appearance of the mound. The cairn has been built up within a series of circular retaining walls, though these cannot now be seen. The chamber is divided into a series of compartments by upright slabs which project from the side-walls; the two end-compartments appear to have been divided horizontally by means of a slab-shelf, but only the supporting stones bonded into the side-walls survive. In the centre of the W wall there is the entrance to a small side-cell; some runes and a bird have been carved on the lintel-stone above the entrance, but the stone is not in its original position.

The tomb was excavated in 1884 by an Orkney antiquary, R S Clouston, and it is remarkable for the number of pottery bowls that were recovered; the type of pottery discovered is now known as Unstan ware. Four leaf-shaped arrowheads and a finely made flint implement were also recorded. Skeletal remains were found in each compartment and two crouched skeletons were discovered in the side cell.

Situation About 4 km NE of Stromness on the Kirkwall road (A 965). OS 1:50,000 map sheet 6; HY 282117.

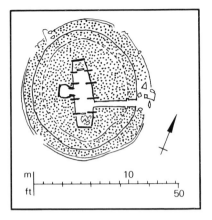

Flint arrowhead from Unstan. (Reproduced by kind permission of the Royal Museum of Scotland)

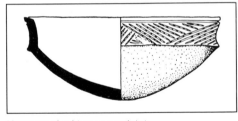

Unstan ware bowl (quarter actual size).

2 Blackhammer Chambered Tomb, Rousay

This cairn is approached by a signposted path on the N side of the Trumland to Westness road and is situated on a shelf on the hillside at a height of about 60 m above sea level. The structure has been covered by a modern concrete roof and only the internal features can now be seen. The cairn is oblong on plan with rounded ends and is composed of two thicknesses of cairn material. The outer face was constructed on a foundation layer of flat slabs and was composed not of horizontally laid dry-stone walling but of slanting slabs in broad interlocking triangles. The inner wall proved to be continuous, although it was less well-preserved at the E end; between three layers of dry-stone walling, the cairn material was composed of rounded stones. The entrance passage was sealed when the cairn was abandoned for burial with carefully laid blocking (access to the tomb is obtained by a ladder through the roof).

The chamber is divided by pairs of upright flagstones into seven compartments; the compartments at each end of the long chamber are independent units, but the five middle compartments comprise pairs of opposing side-stalls with a central passage. The purpose of the masonry in the centre of

22

the chamber (hatched on plan) is not known, although there is no doubt that it is secondary to the construction of the tomb, and the four missing uprights may have been demolished at the same time.

Two skeletons were found during the excavation, one in the entrance passage and the other in the westernmost compartment; in a hollow in the floor of the adjoining compartment were found the remains of a bowl of Unstan ware and a burnt flint knife. Other objects discovered in the chamber include a stone axe and several flint tools. *Situation* On the s coast of the island of Rousay, N of the public road (B 9064). OS 1:50,000 map sheet 6; HY 414276.

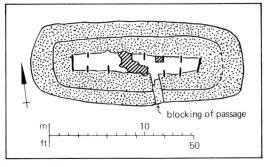

Stone axe from Blackhammer. (Reproduced by kind permission of the Royal Museum of Scotland)

blocking of passage

---

3 Knowe of Yarso Chambered Tomb, Rousay

This cairn is situated on a higher terrace than that of Blackhammer, at a height of about 105 m above sea level, and it is best approached by the signposted route from the Trumland to Westness road. The cairn is rectangular with rounded ends and is made up of two thicknesses of stones held in position within an outer and inner wall with an internal revetment as indicated on the plan. On either side of the entrance, which is at the SE end, the outer dry-stone walling has been laid in slanting courses, a technique which continued round the outer retaining wall of the cairn. A vertical break in the masonry on either side of the passage about 1.2 m from the outside shows the width of the two layers of cairn material at this point.

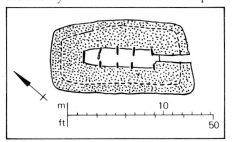

The interior of the tomb is well preserved, and three compartments divided by upright slabs may be seen; the two compartments nearest the entrance comprise pairs of side-stalls. The main compartment, which occupies just less than half of the interior of the chamber, is itself divided by a pair of upright stones to form two side-stalls and an end-stall. A ledge on the NE wall of the end-stall at a height of 1.1 m above ground level may originally have been matched by a similar scarcement on the opposite wall and together they may have been intended to support a shelf.

Excavation showed that the cairn contained the remains of at least twenty-nine individuals, the majority found in the innermost compartment; seventeen were represented only by skulls and fifteen of these were placed side by side at the bottom of the wall with their faces turned inwards. Animal bones from the deposits have been used for radiocarbon analysis, and this indicates that the tomb was in use about 2900 BC.

Situation On the s coast of the island of Rousay, 500 m NNE of the public road (B 9064). OS 1:50,000 map sheet 6; HY 404279.

4   Midhowe Chambered Tomb, Rousay
This cairn, now covered by a vast shed in order to protect the stonework, measured 32.5 m in length and almost 13 m in width; the central chamber, which is almost complete, and the masonry of the casing wall surrounding the cairn make this one of the most instructive of the Orkney monuments. The outer wall-face of the cairn has been carefully executed with a foundation course of flat horizontal slabs; above this the slabs are set at an angle and in the next layer the slabs are laid in the opposite direction to those beneath. The resultant herring-bone pattern is best seen on the E wall. The entrance into the central gallery is at the SE end, and the original blocking is still in position. The chamber, 23.2 m by 2 m, is divided by upright slabs into a series of twelve compartments with a passage running between them. The end compartment is further subdivided by a series of slabs and, like Unstan, may have had a shelf at a height of about 1.1 m above floor level. When covered over, and the side walls still stand to a height of 2.5 m, the central gallery must have been a particularly dark and awe-inspiring vault. In several compartments the burials were placed on or under low stone benches: skeletons were discovered between the fifth and the tenth compartments (counting from the entrance), generally in a crouched position with their backs against the NE wall of the chamber. Some pottery was recovered from the seventh compartment on the SW side of the chamber. The excavators found that the chamber had been deliberately filled with stones in order to prevent further use; but two later crouched burials were discovered in the filling itself (one in a stone cist). *Situation* On the W coast of the island of Rousay close to Midhowe Broch. OS 1:50,000 map sheet 6; HY 372304.

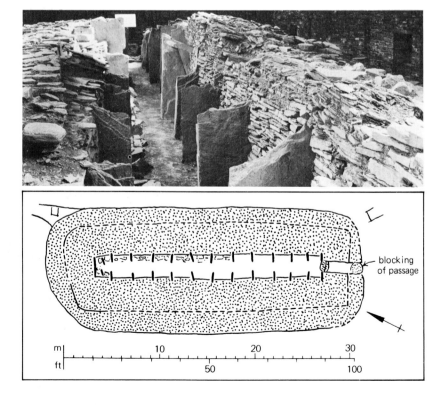

5 Taversoe Tuick Chambered Tomb, Rousay

The two-storied chambered tomb of Taversoe Tuick is an unusual monument, comprising two chambers set one above the other and a small subsidiary chamber built on the perimeter of the site. The lower chamber has been dug into the hillside and was originally entered by a passage on the SE side leading to a roughly rectangular area divided into four compartments by a series of upright slabs. All are provided with shelves, on which skeletal remains, including a crouched burial, were discovered. Three piles of cremated bones had been deposited in the passage. The upper chamber, built immediately above the lower, is entered by a passage from the N side and is completely enclosed by a modern dome; the original cairn was surrounded by a low platform of stones. The central chamber of the upper tomb is divided into two—a small compartment at the NE end, entered between two upright slabs, and the main compartment, which has been further divided by three uprights, though only two of these now survive. There is an unusual straight-sided recess in the SE wall, the purpose of which is not known. When the site was excavated, three stone cists covered by flat slabs were still in position, built on a layer of earth against the N wall of the larger compartment; the cremated remains of several adults and a child were found in these cists. A detached miniature chamber has been dug into the ground some 7.3 m from the cairn on the lower side; pear-shaped on plan, it has been divided by four upright slabs into narrow bays, and the lintelled roof is still intact. Three almost complete pottery bowls were found in the chamber but no burial remains survived. The entrance is now protected by a wooden hatch.

Situation On the S coast of the island of Rousay, 200 m W of Trumland, N of the public road (B 9064). OS 1:50,000 map sheet 6; HY 425276.

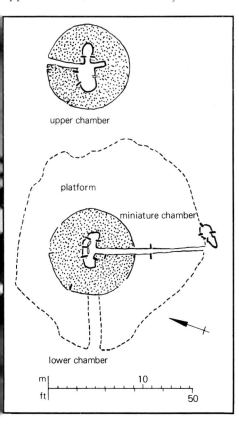

upper chamber

platform

miniature chamber

lower chamber

m | 10
ft | 50

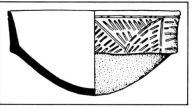

Unstan ware bowl found at Taversoe Tuick (quarter actual size).

25

6 Maes Howe Chambered Tomb, Mainland

The chambered tomb of Maes Howe is one of the greatest architectural achievements of the prehistoric peoples of Scotland; although made possible by the tractable nature of the Orkney flagstones, the conception and craftsmanship of the tomb make it a most remarkable construction. On entering the fenced enclosure the visitor passes through a bank surrounding the site; the lower part of this bank has been shown by excavation to be of prehistoric date. The mound and the flattened area in which it stands are encircled by a shallow ditch. The grass-covered barrow, measuring 35 m in diameter and 7.3 m in height, is composed of clay and angular fragments of rock and encloses the stone-built cairn within which stands the tomb chamber itself. The wall-face of this central core is not vertical, as at Quoyness,

Maes Howe, looking along the entrance passage from the interior.

but has the appearance of a series of steps carefully constructed in dry-stone masonry. It is clear that this central core was not intended to be seen, but is a constructional feature designed to ensure the stability of the chamber. Two retaining walls were also encountered within the barrow and these would have helped to consolidate the mound material. The tough mixture of clay and stones of the mound and the care with which it was heaped up means that Maes Howe retains its original profile even today. Radiocarbon analysis of peat from the bottom of the ditch indicates that the tomb was built sometime before 2700 BC.

The excavation of the chamber was undertaken by J Farrer in 1861 and, as the entrance passage was not negotiable, Farrer made his way into the chamber by means of a shaft driven through the top of the mound. The entrance passage is on the SW side of the mound; the outer part was apparently unroofed, running as a trench through the

skirts of the mound for a distance of about 6.8 m. At this point the passage is roofed and measures about 0.7 m in width and height; the passage then expands to a width of about 0.9 m with a door jamb of about 0.1 m in depth on each side. There is also a step down, which thus increases the height of the passage to 1.4 m. There are two features for the visitor to notice while negotiating the passage; the first is the recess which, it has been suggested, houses the closing stone designed to block the entrance, and the second is the method of construction of the inner part of the passage with monumental side- and roof-slabs. The D-shaped recess on the NW side of the passage just within the entrance is filled by a single stone which could, if manoeuvred between the jambs,

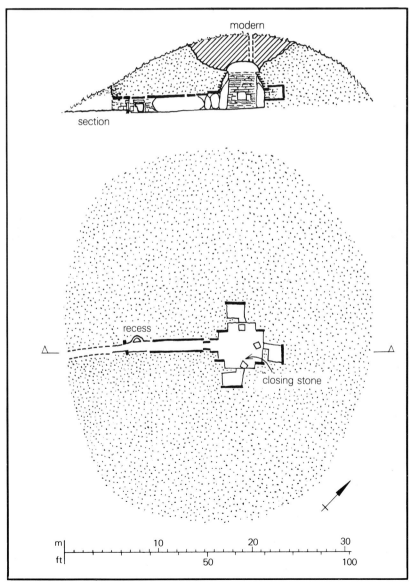

block all but 0.46 m of the entrance. The sides and roof of the passage are made of some of the largest slabs in the tomb, though that on the E side is now fractured; the W side-slab measures no less than 5.6 m in length and the positioning of these three slabs is one of the most impressive engineering feats of the construction. Near the inner end of the passage a pair of pillar-like stones form a slight constriction, the purpose of which is not known.

The initial reaction of the visitor may be that the chamber is smaller than expected, for it takes a moment or two to appreciate the proportions and sense of architectural balance that the builders have achieved. The chamber is some 4.57 m square with a projecting stone buttress in each corner; one side of each buttress is made of a single upright slab and it is perhaps the contrast between these tall pillars and the horizontal dry-stone walls of the chamber that suggests a feeling of space. The buttresses, however, have a very practical purpose, as the walls of the chamber rise vertically for 1.37 m from the floor and then converge gradually to a height of 2.6 m, with the slanting natural fracture of the outer edges of the slabs providing an almost smooth surface. From this point to the surviving height of 3.8 m the walls converge slab by slab to form the square corbelled vault with the buttresses providing important internal support. The upper part of the roof (now painted white) has been reconstructed.

Except for the wall occupied by the passage, there is the entrance to a cell in the centre of each wall, the roofs and backs of which cell are constructed of single slabs, but the other walls are of dry-stone masonry. The cells were probably sealed by the substantial rectangular blocks that now lie in front of their entrances, but these were found on the floor of the chamber and no grave-goods were discovered. Farrer was not the first to break into the tomb, however, for several parties of Norsemen in the mid-twelfth century recorded their presence in the chamber in a series of runic inscriptions, one

These runes, carved by Norsemen in the twelfth century AD, read, in part: 'Happy is he who might find the great treasure'.

of the largest collections of such known, and five of these mention treasure. These have been translated as follows: 'A great treasure is hidden in the north-west'. 'Happy is he who might find the great treasure.' 'It is long ago that a great treasure lay hidden here.' 'Hakon alone bore the treasure out of this mound.' 'It is certain and true as I say, that the treasure has been moved from here. The treasure was taken away three nights before they [opened the mound].' A further inscription reads 'Crusaders opened this mound', and this has sometimes been linked to the removal of the 'treasure' mentioned earlier, but it has recently been pointed out that the two inscriptions are not incised by the same hand. Traditionally the mound is said to have been tenanted by 'Hogboy', the spirit or goblin of great strength that guarded the treasure. While it is an attractive possibility that Maes Howe contained rich and elaborate grave-goods associated with the original burials, the likelihood of gold or silver objects, for only these would the Vikings claim as treasure, is very remote. There is, however, evidence for a rebuilding of the outer bank in the ninth century AD, and this may be a clue to the 'treasure': perhaps the tomb was used for the burial of a Viking chief in the early days of the Norse settlement of Orkney, and it was his treasure that was robbed three centuries later.

Situation About 14.5 km W of Kirkwall on the main Kirkwall to Stromness road (A 965). OS 1:50,000 map sheet 6; HY 318127.

7   Cuween Hill Chambered Tomb, Mainland

This cairn is situated on the NE flank of Cuween Hill, and from it there are extensive views across the Bay of Firth to the E and N. The tomb is entered along a narrow passage, 5.5 m in length and 0.7 m in width, the outer part of which is unroofed, but the inner 3 m are roofed with slabs at a height of only 0.8 m. The flat slabs at the ends appear to be the result of reconstruction, but the vertical slabs are original. The low passage is more difficult to negotiate than most other Orkney tombs, but the high quality of the interior masonry makes it a particularly interesting example. The central chamber is roughly rectangular on plan and the walls still stand to a height of 2.3 m (the roof is modern, for, like Maes Howe, the original excavators made their entry through the top of the mound). The lower parts of the walls are vertical, but the upper courses oversail slightly as they rise. There is a chamber on each side of the central court, each entered through a small opening. The W compartment is divided into two smaller cells, the innermost still covered by its original roof, but the roof of the outer is

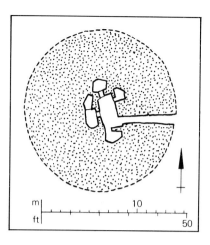

probably a reconstruction. There were the remains of eight inhumation burials, five skulls on the floor of the main chamber and others in the S and W compartments and at the end of the chamber. A large quantity of animal bones was also recovered including an extraordinary, and surely totemic, deposit of twenty-four dog skulls on the floor of the chamber.

Situation About 1.2 km SSE of Finstown. OS 1:50,000 map sheet 6; HY 363127.

8   Wideford Hill Chambered Tomb, Mainland

This cairn is situated on the flank of Wideford Hill, commanding a superb view across the Bay of Firth. The cairn is an almost circular mound of stones and is contained within a carefully constructed dry-stone wall. Two further walls are visible within the cairn structure.

The entrance passage is on the W side; it is slightly curved and it is extremely low and narrow (a trap-door and ladder now provide access to the tomb). There is a well-built rectangular chamber and the over-sailing masonry and the large lintel stones over the cells and passage demonstrate considerable architectural expertise.

Situation 4 km W of Kirkwall on the W slope of Wideford Hill. OS 1:50,000 map sheet 6; HY 409121.

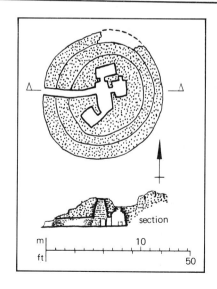

9 Quoyness Chambered Tomb, Sanday
The external appearance of this spectacular tomb is confusing, displaying as it does the complex structure of the cairn. The mound, which stands on an irregular surrounding platform and measures 20.4 m by 17 m and at least 4.3 m in height, is contained within three wall-faces. The inner wall encloses the chamber and cells, while the median wall provides the main outline of the cairn. The outer wall-face, which is continuous in front of the entrance, may be connected with the final blocking of the tomb rather than with its use as a monument for collective burial.

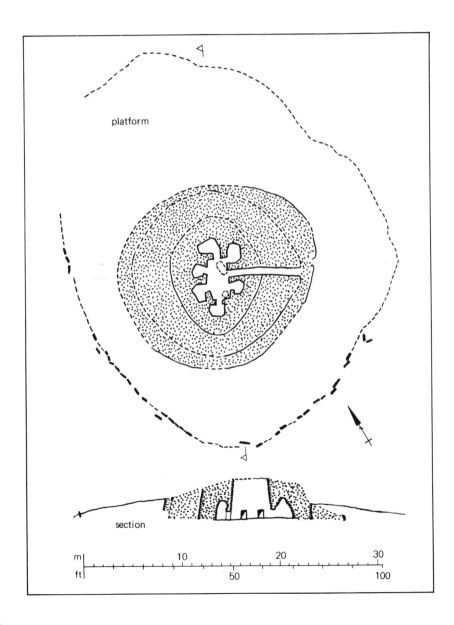

platform

section

| m | | 10 | | 20 | | 30 |
| ft | | | 50 | | | 100 |

The entrance to the chamber is on the SE side of the cairn; the precise arrangement is not clear, as it seems to have been disturbed as a result of the nineteenth-century excavation. At the end of the passage and at right angles to it, the spacious main chamber still stands to a height of about 4 m. The walls rise vertically for the first metre at which point they converge to decrease the final span of the roof to 3.3 m by 0.86 m. When the cairn was excavated two features were found in the floor of the main chamber: a circular stone-lined cist in the S corner and an oval depression in the NE corner. The cist

The interior of the chambered tomb at Quoyness on Sanday.

contained the fragmentary skeletal remains of at least ten adults and four or five children, but there were no skeletal remains in the oval depression.

Six irregular cells are entered from the main chamber, and skulls and bones were found in all but two of them (the two in the opposite wall from the passage). Excavation also produced a polished bone pin with a projection on one side and a polished slate object, shaped rather like a hammer head, both of which can be paralleled among the finds from Skara Brae. Radiocarbon analysis of human bones suggests that the tomb was in use around 2900 BC.

Situation On the E side of the peninsula known as Els Ness on the S coast of the island of Sanday; it is about 4 km from the airstrip. OS 1:50,000 map sheet 5; HY 676378.

Bone pin and stone objects found in the chambered tomb at Quoyness (half actual size).

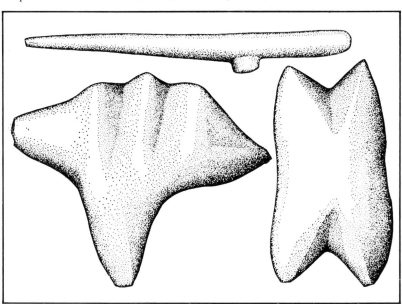

10   Holm of Papa Westray Chambered Tomb

Holm of Papa Westray is a small island off the E side of Papa Westray, separated from it by the bay of South Wick. On the highest part of the island the long mound of the chambered cairn is a conspicuous landmark, and near the N tip of the island there is a recently excavated stalled cairn (not in state care).

The long cairn of the Maes Howe type tomb is about 35 m long and 16.8 m broad and is now covered by a concrete roof to protect the chamber and cells, and the visitor enters through a hatch in the roof. The original entrance-passage is in the centre of the SE side and leads to the central chamber, and there are subsidiary chambers at either end, themselves cut off by cross-walls. On plan the layout of the central chamber and side-cells may seem at some remove from the architectural exactness of Maes Howe, but the masonry of the chamber is of a high order; the lowest 1.5 m is vertical, and then the side-walls converge to narrow the roofing span. There are three low entrances to side-cells on each side of the main chamber—two of these cells, in opposing corners of the chamber, being double. There are three cells each in the subsidiary chambers—the layout of these conforming to the Maes Howe type.

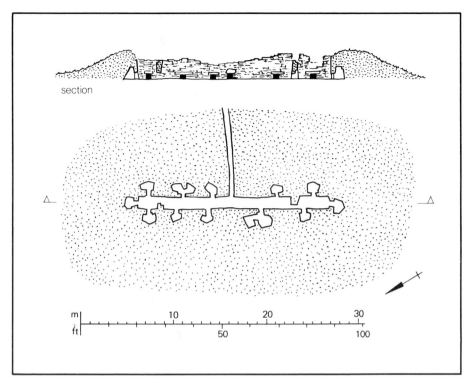

section

An unusual feature of this tomb is the presence of a number of stones decorated by the original users of the tomb; the lintel above the SE cell is decorated with several depressions, two 'eye-brow' motifs and a symbol not unlike the letters EO. On the opposite wall a zig-zag and a series of almost circular motifs have been carved. On the SE side-wall of the main chamber, about 1.5 m S of the entrance-passage and at a height of 1.4 m, there is a fractured stone with what has been a double ring and conjoined pecked circles with central dots.

Situation On the SE side of the island of Holm of Papa Westray. OS 1:50,000 map sheet 5; HY 509518.

A decorated stone in the chambered tomb on the Holm of Papa Westray.

11 The Dwarfie Stane, Hoy

The Dwarfie Stane is situated on the E side of the valley which runs across the N end of Hoy between Quoys and Rackwick; it is an isolated block of red sandstone on a terrace which commands views both towards Mainland, to the N, and the sea, to the SW. The stone measures 8.5 m in length, up to 4.5 m in breadth and 2 m in height.

On the W side of the stone there is a rock-cut entrance giving access to a short passage with further openings to a cell on either side. A large block of similar dimensions to the entrance lies in front of it and was formerly employed to seal the passage; it was certainly still in position in the sixteenth century, and it may be that the breach in the roof of the chamber was caused during an attempt to break into the tomb while it was blocked by this stone, but this hole has now been skilfully restored. There is another possible entrance-stone a few metres behind the Dwarfie Stane. The cells are divided from the central area by distinct kerbs forming carefully squared doorways into the rounded cells. At the E end of the south cell there is a low ridge of rock which has been described as a pillow. This is a remarkable monument because of its situation, careful construction and its part in recent folklore; Norna of Fitful Head in Scott's *The Pirate* describes 'this extraordinary dwelling, which Trolld, a dwarf famous in the northern Sagas, is said to have framed for his own favourite residence'.

The Dwarfie Stane is now regarded as a rock-cut chambered tomb of local inspiration rather than of Mediterranean derivation, and the layout of the passage and cells may be seen as a simplification of the lower chambers of Taversoe Tuick on Rousay. *Situation* About 4 km from the landing place at Mo Ness in the N part of the island of Hoy. OS 1:50,000 map sheet 6; HY 243004.

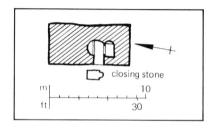

closing stone

m ⌐_____10
ft ⌐_____30

The Dwarfie Stane on Hoy.

34

12 Knap of Howar, Neolithic Settlement, Papa Westray

The small island of Papa Westray in the north of the Orkneys has long been recognised as a place which attracted early settlement. It was part of an important Norse family estate in the eleventh and twelfth centuries. But long before that, in the third and fourth millennia BC, the island was known to the neolithic Orcadians who built the chambered tombs on the Holm of Papa Westray. The prime attraction of Papa Westray to these early peoples was undoubtedly its soil, which is unusually rich and fertile.

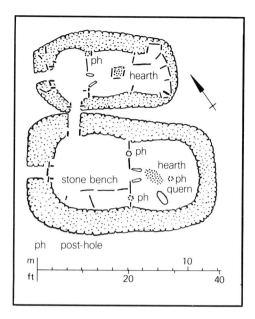

On the west coast of the island, facing across Papa Sound to the north end of Westray, there are the remains of two stone-built houses lying side by side. They are known by the somewhat tautological name of Knap of Howar which is derived from Old Norse and means 'knob of the mounds'; before excavation, the site was covered by irregular sand hillocks and the name would have been appropriate. The two buildings survive in an unusually good state of preservation—the walls still stand to a maximum height of 1.62 m and two doorways are still intact.

Knap of Howar was inhabited more than five thousand years ago; radiocarbon analysis of animal bones left as food debris by the inhabitants showed that the houses had been built sometime between about 3700 and 2800 BC. It is in fact the earliest known settlement in the Orkneys, and the material culture of its inhabitants shows very clearly that they belonged to the same group of people who built chambered tombs of the Orkney-Cromarty class. A large quantity of pottery was recovered, much of it coarse and undistinguished but some belongs to the Unstan type of fine decorated bowls which occurs in several chambered tombs.

The site had been occupied before, though only shortly before, the surviving stone houses were built, for the domestic debris of an earlier phase of settlement lies beneath their walls. A layer of midden about half a metre thick covers a large area to either side of the houses; when the houses were built, the requisite space was cleared of midden so that the floor was clean natural subsoil and the walls were built on a foundation of midden. The material scraped up from inside the houses was then used to fill the wall-core, between inner and outer skins of dry-stone masonry. When excavated, the midden proved to be rich in artefacts and food debris. Apart from abundant sherds of pottery, implements made of flint, stone and bone were found.

Flint was made into implements which needed sharp edges, such as scrapers for preparing animal skins, leaf-shaped points and a simple knife, and large beach pebbles were collected and used as hammers and pounders. Bone awls were found, which could be used for making holes in leather in order to fashion clothes—weaving was unknown in Scotland at this period. These are all common everyday objects, but Knap of Howar has also yielded more unusual equipment including a small polished stone axe, whalebone mallets and a finely shaped whalebone spatula, and unique forms of

35

stone borers and grinders. The economy of the settlement seems to have depended primarily on stock-breeding, fishing, hunting, and gathering shellfish, but the inhabitants were also growing cereal crops. Domestic and wild animals included cattle, sheep, pigs and deer, and their bones were mixed up in the midden with vast quantities of shells of oyster, limpet, whelk and razor-fish, which were evidently quite an important element in the diet of the inhabitants.

The larger of the two buildings, House 1, appears to have been the main dwelling-house. It was divided into two rooms by a low partition of upright stone slabs and two timber posts which also helped to support the roof. The outer room was partially paved with flagstones and it was furnished with a low stone bench along one wall; heating came from an open hearth just beyond the stone partition. This inner room, in which the hearth lay, had an earthen floor and seems to have functioned as a kitchen or working area. Two stone querns were found here, one of which is still in position beside the wall; when excavated the original rubbing stones were found beside this massive saddle quern, together with a pile of

crushed razor-shells. As some of the pottery contains small fragments of razor-shell as grit in the clay, it is possible that crushing the shells was at least one of the functions of the great quern. Traces of the bedding grooves for wooden benches were found along both side-walls of this workroom, and a small cupboard is visible in the N wall.

The smaller building to the N, House 2, was furnished with several cupboards and storage compartments and it was divided into three small rooms by stone partitions. This building proved to have been built slightly later than House 1—probably as extra storage and working space. Two successive hearths were found in the central room; the earlier hearth, which is still visible, was kerbed and lined with stone slabs, while the later hearth was set in a shallow hollow in the floor.

Situation On the W coast of the island of Papa Westray, 800 m W of Holland House. OS 1:50,000 map sheet 5; HY 483518.

House 2 at Knap of Howar is divided into three by partitions; to the left are a row of wall cupboards.

13 Skara Brae, Neolithic Settlement, Mainland

On the shore of Skaill Bay on the west coast of the mainland of Orkney is one of the most remarkable monuments in Britain. There are the houses and alleyways of a small village which was flourishing on the edge of the then known world around four and a half thousand years ago. And these are not just foundations that survive; in some cases the walls of the houses stand to eaves level and alleyways are still roofed over with the original stone slabs. During its lifetime, the settlement became embedded in its own rubbish heaps and, after it was abandoned, it became choked with sand. The combination of refuse and sand has preserved the buildings and debris of everyday life to a unique degree and, because timber was scarce and good stone available, even the furniture inside the houses was built in stone and still survives.

Not surprisingly, Skara Brae has attracted a good deal of attention since its discovery around 1850 and it has been excavated on no less than six occasions. The major excavations took place in the late 1920s and the details of the settlement then uncovered are described in the official guide-book available at the site, where there is also a small museum. Evidence of at least four periods of building activity was found and it is clear that people were living here continuously over several generations, dismantling old dwellings and building new ones as the need arose. Their material culture remained much the same throughout; the last inhabitants had been using essentially the same sort of pottery vessels as their ancestors who founded the settlement. The maximum number of houses at any one period seems to have been six to eight and it is probable that there were no more than 40 to 50 people in the community.

Skara Brae was again the scene of archaeological activity in 1972 and 1973 when small scale excavations were carried out not on the buildings but on the rubbish deposits around them. In the intervening forty or so years since the earlier excavations, archaeology had adopted many new scientific techniques which allow far more information to be retrieved from the surviving debris of prehistoric life than was possible earlier. Modern techniques could provide answers to many vital questions

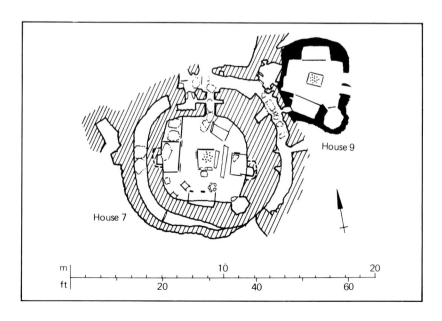

House 9

House 7

m   10   20

ft   20   40   60

about the date and economic life of the settlement—questions such as what the inhabitants ate and how they exploited the resources of their environment. With this end in view, two areas of kitchen midden left untouched by earlier operations were excavated; one lay in the central part of the settlement in the space enclosed by Passages F, A and B and House 7 (these structures are marked on the plan in the site guide-book), while the other lay on the NW edge of the visible settlement by the present entrance to the site. The latter area proved to have been used only sporadically for dumping rubbish, for the refuse layers were inter-leaved with layers of natural wind-blown sand, but one of the lower and earlier middens was extremely damp, with the result that some very exciting organic remains had been preserved, including fragments of wooden objects and small pieces of rope. There was also an abundance of plant remains; moss,

sedge and grass were recognisable and there were seeds of the campion family and pollen from dandelion and plantain. Full analysis of this material is still in progress at the time of writing.

The central area of midden excavated in 1972-3 was rich in artefacts and food debris to a massive depth of 4.3 m. Bones of wild and domesticated animals, birds and fish were found, as were marine shellfish—especially limpets. Burnt grain suggests that the people of Skara Brae were agriculturalists as well as animal-breeders and fishermen. Apart from yielding information about the economic aspects of the settlement, the animal bones were also used for radiocarbon analysis. A series of radiocarbon dates was obtained and suggests that the settlement was occupied between about 3200 BC and 2200 BC.

Situation 10.2 km N of Stromness (A 967 and B 9056) and about 25.5 km NW of Kirkwall (A 965 and B 9055). OS 1:50,000 map sheet 6; HY 231187.

Skara Brae and the Bay of Skaill.

14 Stones of Stenness, Mainland

The twin promontories between the Lochs of Stenness and Harray, now linked by the narrow Bridge of Brodgar, contain two of the most evocative of the megalithic monuments of Orkney—the Stones of Stenness and the Ring of Brodgar. These stone circles are visible from many places (one of the best views is from the top of Staney Hill), and from the sites themselves there are panoramic views of the Mainland hills and of the steep cliffs of the island of Hoy.

The henge monument of the Stones of Stenness is the earlier site, constructed probably in the early third millennium BC and, impressive though the surviving standing stones are, the original appearance of the site must have been even more splendid. There were probably twelve standing stones in the original plan surrounded by a deep rock-cut ditch and by a substantial bank. There was a single entrance-causeway through the ditch and bank on the N side of the site. Of the existing standing stones the most southerly pair have been in position since they were set up; the other tall stone stood until 1814 when the tenant farmer felled it and broke the adjacent stone into pieces. The crooked northerly

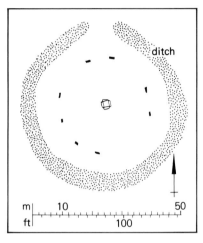

The Stones of Stenness. The Watch Stone stands in the background.

stone was first found in 1906 during the work involved with the re-erection of the fallen stone when the site was taken into state care, and the newly discovered stone was also set upright at this time. The stumps of four other stones are known to exist although only one is now visible; the holes for two other stones were recorded in the course of excavation in 1973, as was the likely position of the twelfth, although there were no traces of the stump. The standing stones were set in holes larger than the girth of the stones and up to about 1 m in depth and the holes were then filled with boulders to support the uprights.

This stone setting was found in the centre of the Stones of Stenness during excavations in 1973.

At the centre of the circle there is an almost square setting of stones laid horizontally into the subsoil. This setting contained tiny fragments of cremated bone, charcoal and sherds of grooved ware pottery, mixed with earth and small stones. Between the centre of the circle and the entrance two upright stones and a stone now lying flat are the remains of a further setting; although put together to form a table-like structure in 1907, the original layout of these stones is not certain.

There are two outlying standing stones which may be associated with the Stones of Stenness and there were formerly two others; the Barnhouse Stone is situated 700 m SE and the Watch Stone 170 m NNW. The former stands within a cultivated field and close access to it may not always be possible, but it is a shapely stone and may be viewed from the roadside. The Watch Stone is the only survivor of three stones which were situated at the northern end of the promontory; it is a huge straight-sided monolith 5.6 m in height. The stump of another stone was found some 14 m SSW of the Watch Stone in 1930 but it has since been removed. To the N of the Stones of Stenness and to the E of the Watch Stone was the site of the Stone of Odin; this was broken and removed at the same time as the felling of two of the stones of the Stenness circle. The stone was about 2.4 m in height and has a particular fascination in Orcadian folklore for it was perforated by a hole at a height of about 1.5 m above ground level. 'Up to the time of its destruction, it was customary to leave some offering on visiting the stone, such as a piece of bread, or cheese, or a rag, or even a stone; but a still more romantic character was associated with this pillar, for it was considered that a promise made while the plighting parties grasped their hands through the hole was peculiarly sacred.'

Archaeology cannot answer the question 'What do these stones mean?', but the visitor walking between the Stones of Stenness and the Ring of Brodgar, passing the Watch Stone and two further uprights to the SE of the farm of Brodgar, may have the impression of following a ceremonial way. The Ness of Brodgar was certainly a place of burial in the second millennium BC for at least five cists were discovered in ploughing in 1925, four of them lying parallel to one another in a line running north and south; overlapping two of the cists was a slab decorated with lozenges, chevrons and other linear motifs. There was formerly a cairn or mound in the same field as the two standing stones but it has been considerably despoiled in recent centuries.

Situation The Stones of Stenness are on the SE shore of the Loch of Stenness on the E side of the B 9055 and 600 m NW of its junction with the Kirkwall to Stromness road (A 965). OS 1:50,000 map sheet 6; HY 306125.

15   Ring of Brodgar, Mainland

The Ring of Brodgar is the focus of the second major group of monuments in this area, which comprises imposing barrows, the Comet Stone and the henge monument and stone circle. The deep ditch that surrounds the stone circle is broken by two opposing causeways, one in the NW and the other in the SE quadrant of the circle. Like that at the Stones of Stenness, the Brodgar ditch was cut into the solid bedrock, and excavation has revealed that it was originally as much as 3 m in depth and 9 m across; because there has been no ploughing across the ditch or the interior of the circle, the ditch has not been so severely filled by soil as that at the Stones of Stenness. The Ring of Brodgar is an unusual henge monument as there is no surviving outer bank, and the central area is thus cut off only by the surrounding ditch.

There were originally sixty stones in the circle and these were set six degrees apart from geographical north; the circle was carefully laid out apparently using a standard unit of length of 2.72 feet (the Megalithic

The Ring of Brodgar from the air. The encircling ditch is broken by causeways to right and left. Beyond the Ring lie several burial mounds. (Reproduced by kind permission of the Royal Commission on the Ancient and Historical Monuments of Scotland)

yard) and the diameter of 340 feet is 125 Megalithic yards or 50 Megalithic rods (1 rod = 2.5 M yards). Only thirty-six stones remain in position, either as uprights or broken stumps, but there is little doubt about the mathematics of the layout of the circle. Several of the stones, particularly on the N side of the circle, are supported by chocking stones set at right angles to the upright, and now just protruding above the turf. The stones are undecorated except for a series of Norse runes and a cross on a broken upright in the northern quadrant; the runes, like some in Maes Howe, form a cryptogram, here giving a common name, Bjorn. The interior of the circle has not been excavated.

On the SE of the circle there are numerous small mounds but, although some of them appear to have been excavated in the past,

41

nothing is known of their contents. There are two more impressive mounds, one on the s lip of the henge ditch and the other, known as Salt Knowe, situated 100 m sw of the henge; a cist has been revealed in the latter, but neither mound has been fully excavated. To the E of the Ring of Brodgar stands the monolith known as the Comet Stone; it is set on a low platform (13 m in diameter) and the stumps of two other stones are visible. Close to the shore of the Loch of Harray are two large mounds, the more northerly of which has been described as 'Plumcake Barrow'. In the 1850s a trench was cut through the centre of the mound about 2.7 m in width; two cists were discovered, one of them containing a steatite cinerary urn with cremated bones. The second cist held a pottery vessel also with a cremation deposit, but the pot 'almost immediately fell to pieces on being exposed to the atmosphere'. Some excavation was also undertaken on the more southerly barrow but the results were inconclusive, and it is not clear how much, if any, of the mound is artificial.

It has recently been suggested that the circle and the mounds round about it form a lunar observatory from which variations in

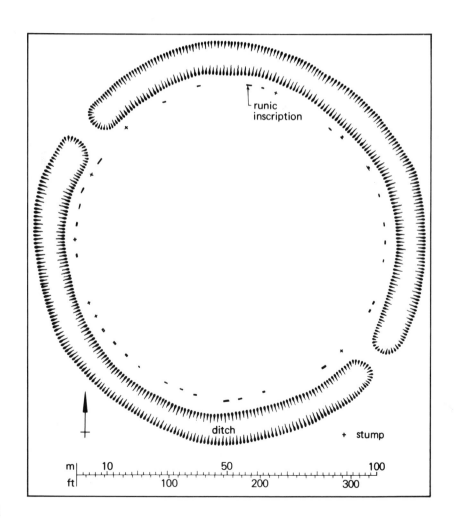

runic inscription

ditch   + stump

m | 10   50   100
ft | 100   200   300

42

the moon's movements could be examined from three positions. The date at which the barrows could have been used in this way has been calculated to be about 1560 BC plus or minus 100 in calendar years. It is likely that the construction of the circle is earlier than this and, without excavation, the date of the barrows cannot be determined. It is thus impossible at present to prove whether or not this attractive theory is correct.

Situation The Ring of Brodgar lies between the Lochs of Stenness and Harray on the W side of the B 9055 and 1.5 km NW of the Stones of Stenness. OS 1:50,000 map sheet 6; HY 294133.

A section across the ditch of the Ring of Brodgar excavated in 1973. (Photograph by Nick Bradford reproduced by kind permission of Professor A C Renfrew)

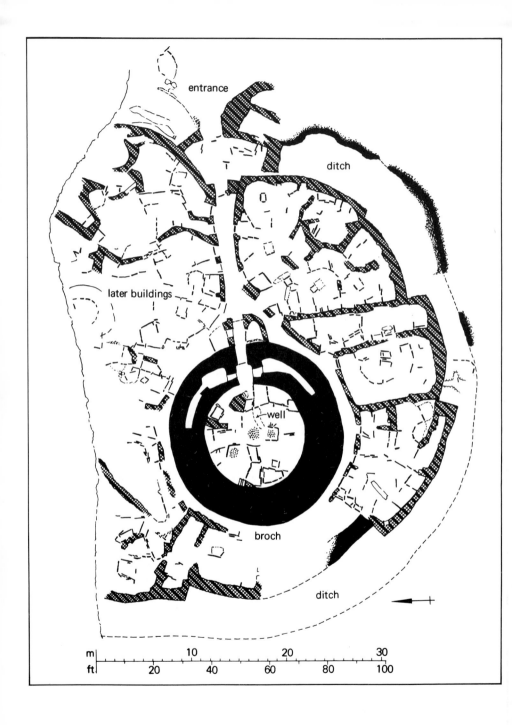

entrance

ditch

later buildings

well

broch

ditch

| m | | 10 | | 20 | | 30 |
| ft | 20 | 40 | 60 | 80 | 100 |

16 Gurness Broch, Mainland

The broch of Gurness stands on the tip of a promontory known as Aikerness on the E coast of mainland, and its situation emphasises the importance of the sea to its prehistoric builders. At one time the entire site was covered by a large mound but excavations were begun in 1929, gradually revealing a broch and a complex of contemporary and later buildings, and the site is now open to view as an exceptional illustration of almost continuous settlement from the turn of the Christian era until the Viking Age. A guide-leaflet is available from the site museum, which houses a selection of the objects found in the course of excavation.

Like most brochs in the Northern Isles, Gurness was built with a thick stone base to the tower, which made it possible for the walls to rise to a considerable height. The surviving masonry is incomplete, owing to collapse and stone-robbing, but the tower

The Broch of Gurness with part of its adjacent settlement in the foreground. Beyond lies the island of Rousay.

might well have risen originally to a height of some 12 m or more. The broch was encircled by three lines of ditch and rampart with an entrance causeway at the E, though much of these early defences and buildings have been destroyed by coastal erosion to the north of the broch. The precise date at which the broch was built is unknown but by analogy with brochs elsewhere it is likely to have been in the first century BC. By the third century AD the broch-tower had lost its original defensive character and had been converted into a domestic dwelling. The external buildings are complex and difficult to interpret in detail but they are characterised by dry-stone masonry of a high quality, by the use of upright slabs as partitions and by carefully constructed rectilinear hearths. The latest houses were built on top of the structures still standing on the s side of the broch and were removed and rebuilt outside the fortified area when the site was excavated; they consist of a five-celled house and part of an oblong building and they are likely to date to the later first millennium AD. It has been

suggested, but cannot be proved, that the oblong building was a Norse long house. Certainly there was Norse activity on the site in the ninth century AD, for the grave of a well-to-do woman was discovered in the upper core of the inner rampart on the N or seaward side of the entrance-causeway. She had been buried in a roughly constructed stone-lined pit, lying on her back with her head to the W, and some of her personal belongings had been placed in the grave with her. At her breast there were two large oval brooches made of bronze; they form a matching pair with elaborate openwork decoration. On the corroded back of one of these brooches were discovered traces of fabric which showed that the body had been dressed in finely woven wool. An iron necklet hung round her neck, a small iron sickle lay at her right side and a knife with a wooden handle at her left (these finds are in Tankerness House Museum in Kirkwall).

Indications of another historical people, the Picts, were found at Gurness in the form of a bone knife-handle incised with an ogam

A brooch found in a Norse grave at Gurness.

inscription and a stone lightly carved with Pictish symbols—the latter may be seen in the site museum. A fragment of another Pictish symbol-stone was recently found in the sands of Evie just to the NW of the site. *Situation* About 27.4 km NW of Kirkwall (A 965 and 966) and just over 1 km NE of Evie pier where there is a car park. OS 1:50,000 map sheet 6; HY 381268.

17 Midhowe Broch, Rousay

The shores of Eynhallow Sound abound with the remains of brochs, both along the coast of the mainland and along the Rousay shore, and they must have been a daunting sight in their original condition. The broch of Midhowe stands in a particularly fine situation on a very rocky shore with a narrow creek or geo on either side, so that it occupies in effect a promontory. The landward side is barred by a formidable triple line of defence, consisting of two ditches with a massive stone wall set between them. The broch itself survives to a height of 4.3 m, with a ledge or scarcement on the inner face of the wall which carried a first-floor gallery at a height of about 3.3 m. The broch wall has an internal gallery at ground-level, an unusual feature among the normally solid-based brochs of the Northern Isles, and the effect of this hollow base was to weaken the broch; at some stage in its occupation the ground

gallery had to be blocked partially when the wall threatened to collapse. The wall was also buttressed on the outside by stone slabs set on end and side by side. The broch is almost circular, with an overall diameter of about 18 m and an internal diameter of about 9.6 m.

The doorway into the broch faces out to sea rather than towards the land, and it is possible that the Geo of Brough, which it overlooks and which is the broader of the two creeks flanking the site, was the main landing-place for boats. The doorway itself is well preserved and impressive, allowing more headroom than many broch entrances. There are two door-checks, one at the inner end of the entrance passage and one at a distance of about 2.3 m from the outer end, and between the two lie openings into cells built within the thickness of the wall. The cell on the right of the entrance has an excellent corbelled roof, while the left-hand cell opens into the intra-mural gallery which runs

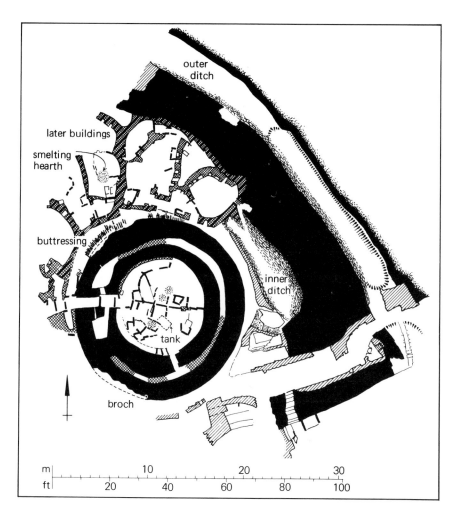

later buildings

smelting
hearth

buttressing

outer
ditch

inner
ditch

tank

broch

m		10		20		30
ft	20	40	60	80	100

round inside the broch wall almost to the back of the other cell. There was originally an upper mural gallery as well, to which access was gained by a stairway opening from inside the broch but at a height of 1.7 m above the broch-floor, which suggests the use of a wooden ladder.

The inside of the broch is confusingly full of slab partitions, alcoves, hearths, and tanks, most of which represent secondary rather than original building activities. A stone-kerbed hearth slightly to the right of centre on entering possesses a carefully constructed stone socket on either side which would probably have held the uprights for a

spit across the fire. Beside and slightly overlapped by the hearth there is a fine stone tank with a well-fitting slab-lid; this was a water-tank supplied by good spring water which still flows up through a crack in the rock. Against the broch wall to the left on entering there is the product of a remarkable feat of dry-stone building: an alcove has been formed by a large slab, almost 2.3 m tall, set on end and supporting a pier of dry-stone masonry, which soars up and becomes a corbelled roof over the alcove.

There was once an extensive complex of secondary buildings partially surrounding the broch tower but this has suffered from

47

The Broch of Midhowe from the air. The staircase within the thickness of the broch wall is clearly visible. Between the broch and its landward defences to the left lie a group of houses. The sea (to the right) has probably destroyed other houses but the site is now protected by a wall.

coastal erosion. Only one building survives complete; it was built in the space between the tower and the massive defensive wall to the N and its plan is shaped accordingly. This area of the original inner ditch has been filled in and part of the inner face of the rampart wall removed in order to build an irregular structure consisting of three main compartments. There are signs of considerable modification to the building over the years, but the various cubicles,

recesses and doorways provide a graphic impression of the domestic background of the post-broch era.

Two cup-marked stones were utilised in the course of building operations; one was incorporated into the NE outer face of the broch-tower and shows ring-marks as well, and the other, bearing cup-marks alone, was built into a stretch of late walling to the SE of the tower.

Many artefacts were found during the excavation of Midhowe, mostly domestic equipment but with a few surprises. Among the latter were fragments of a bronze patera or ladle and some sherds of pottery, all of which have a Roman origin and must have reached Midhowe as a result of raiding or trading expeditions to the south. Lumps of iron slag and the remains of a smelting hearth in one of the secondary buildings to the N of the broch-tower demonstrate that iron-working was carried out on the site, although no iron artefacts have survived. Bronze-working was also a local activity, for fragments of crucibles and moulds used in casting bronze objects were found. Three ring-headed pins and three penannular brooches made of bronze indicate the type of fastenings that were used in personal dress,

and a number of stone and bone spindle whorls show that some garments at least were woven, perhaps using long-handled combs made of whalebone to beat down the threads on the loom. Most of the objects recovered were made either of bone or stone and they represent a wide range of everyday tools from bone awls to whetstones and querns.

Situation On the W coast of the island of Rousay about 8 km from Trumland pier. OS 1:50,000 map sheet 6; HY 371306.

18 Grain Earth-house, Mainland

This particularly fine earth-house on the outskirts of modern Kirkwall was discovered around 1827, but the site was filled in again until 1857 when an antiquary dug into it, unfortunately leaving very little record of what he found. There appear to have been remains of walls and domestic refuse at

ground-level above and alongside the earth-house, representing the surface settlement to which it belonged, but no artefacts were found either then or at the time of its original discovery.

The earth-house consists of chamber and passage in the normal way but in addition there is the unusual feature of a flight of steps

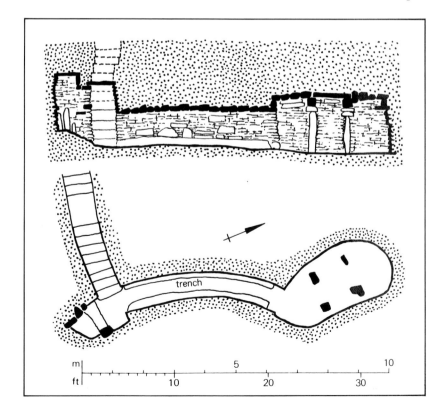

leading from ground-level down into the end of the passage. The upper part of the stair was rebuilt when the site was taken into state care in 1908, but the lower part is original. The passage runs in a pronounced curve until it opens out into a bean-shaped chamber; unlike the earth-house at Rennibister, the roof of the chamber is not corbelled but lintelled in the same way as the passage. The

slabs are supported at a height of about 1.5 m by four free-standing piers built of single upright stones and, where necessary to increase their height, smaller stones on top. Both chamber and passage are carefully built of dry-stone masonry, and they were quite empty when first explored. A second earth-house and remains of ground-level buildings were found nearby in 1982, and it seems likely that both earth-houses were once part of a single domestic settlement.

Situation 800 m NW of Kirkwall harbour (A 965). OS 1:50,000 map sheet 6; HY 441116.

The interior of the earth-house at Grain.

19 Rennibister Earth-house, Mainland

On 12 November 1926 part of the farmyard at Rennibister collapsed beneath the weight of a threshing machine. This exposed an underground chamber whose roof had given way, and this remarkable monument, still in the midst of a farmyard, has been reconstructed where necessary and made accessible to the public. It is one of the most skilfully built of the known Orcadian earth-houses (also known as souterrains); the walls are constructed in dry-stone masonry curving inwards to form a corbelled roof over the oval chamber. Extra support for the roof (and the earth above it) is provided by four pillars, each made of a single stone slab, and five small recesses, rather like open cupboards, have been built into the walls, one at floor-level and the others just above the floor.

Original access to the chamber was gained not through the roof but down a gently sloping passage, with a rough step at the chamber entrance to break the drop down to the floor of the chamber. The walls of the passage have a basal course of upright stones and horizontal dry-stone masonry above, rising to a lintelled roof at a height of 0.7 m; only 0.6 m wide, this narrow entrance-way runs for 3.5 m apparently to a dead end, but presumably entry was designed through the roof at the passage-end where the lintels give way to a well-like cavity utilised by a modern hatchway.

When the earth-house was first discovered, the entrance to the passage was choked with domestic refuse—cockle and whelk shells mixed with black earth—but the rest of the passage and the chamber were free of debris. The chamber itself contained a mass of disarticulated human bones on the floor. The bones represented six adults and about twelve children of various ages and their presence in the earth-house is a mystery. Rennibister is the only Orcadian earth-house to have yielded burials of any sort, and it is clear from the disarticulated nature of the bones that the bodies had been stored elsewhere before being deposited in the earth-house. It is most unlikely that Rennibister was designed as a burial vault; whatever event is reflected by the human bones, their deposition here was secondary, and presumably final, in the life of the earth-house.

Situation 6.5 km WNW of Kirkwall (A 965). OS 1:50,000 map sheet 6; HY 397125.

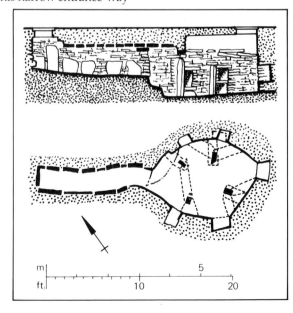

51

20 The Brough of Birsay, Early Christian and Norse Settlements, Mainland

At the NW tip of the mainland of Orkney there lies a most beautiful grass-covered island known as the Brough of Birsay. It is only about 21 ha in extent, rising to high steep cliffs on the west, where puffins live, and sloping gently towards the shore on the E side where it faces the mainland. It is a tidal island and can be reached on foot at low tide across an artificial causeway. At the foot of the slope on the E side of the island are the remains of an extensive and unusually interesting settlement of Early Christian and Viking times. A detailed guide-book is available and there is a small site-museum containing a selection of objects found during the excavations.

The earliest settlement on the Brough was

The Pictish and Norse settlement on the Brough of Birsay from the air. In the centre lies the church and its surrounding enclosure. In the background and in the foreground are the houses of the Norse settlement. (Reproduced by kind permission of the Royal Commission on the Ancient and Historical Monuments of Scotland)

ecclesiastical and belonged to the Celtic Church. Little survived beneath later buildings, but a churchyard or enclosure has been identified, surrounded by a curving wall and containing a series of buildings and graves. Traces of earlier walling beneath the S side of the later nave may represent the church or chapel belonging to the Celtic settlement. Among the graves, many of which are still visible, there is a remarkable sculptured monument; it is a Pictish symbol stone which was broken when discovered and bears splendid carvings of abstract symbols and human figures. There are three bearded warriors, armed with square shields and spears, and above them are carved an eagle, a fantasy beast sometimes known as the 'swimming elephant' and two symbols (the crescent and V-rod, and the mirror case). The original stone is now in the Royal Museum of Scotland, Queen Street, Edinburgh; a copy stands in place on the site.

Most of the visible remains belong to the Viking Age or later. Superimposed on the earlier churchyard is the ruin of a fine early

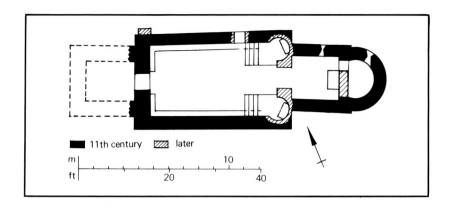

11th century ▨ later

m   10
ft   20   40

twelfth-century church with its accompanying graves and rectangular cemetery wall. There are also extensive domestic buildings of the Norse and later periods. On the seaward side of the church excavation has revealed a complex of buildings, mostly dating to the tenth and eleventh centuries and showing a long history of alteration and rebuilding, the detailed history of which is unclear. The range of rooms known as 'Earl Thorfinn's Palace' includes an impressive bath-house. Part of a boat slipway may be seen at the cliff edge and the extent of the erosion which has

occurred since the Viking Age may be judged by the height above the beach at which the slipway now peters out.

Other houses are visible on the slope behind the ecclesiastical complex, including some of the finest examples of Norse hall-houses ever found in Scotland. These are the typical family houses of the Norsemen and consist essentially of a single long hall, furnished with benches on either side of a hearth and built of stone and turf.

Situation At the NW point of Mainland, 32 km NW of Kirkwall (A 965 and 986). OS 1:50,000 map sheet 6; HY 239285.

Brooch mould from the excavations on the Brough of Birsay.

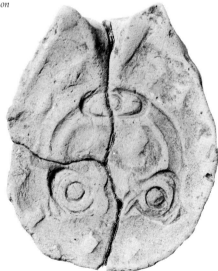

53

21 Cubbie Roo's Castle, Wyre

Standing on the crest of a small ridge along the west side of the island of Wyre are the remains of a castle. Built to a simple though sturdy design, it displays no distinctive features that can be used to date its construction at all closely, but it is generally accepted to be a Norse castle of the mid-twelfth century and as such it is a rare and exciting monument.

Orkneyinga Saga records that, in the mid-twelfth century, Wyre was the home of an outstanding Norwegian named Kolbein Hruga, who built a fine stone castle as a safe stronghold for himself and his family. It was such a strong castle that the assassins of Earl John Haraldson sought refuge there in 1231 and were able to resist attack from the earl's avenging friends. The only trace of any such castle on Wyre is the ruin known as Cubbie Roo's Castle. The name Cubbie Roo is a corruption of Kolbein Hruga, for Kubbie or Kobbie was a Norse nickname for Kolbein. The fact that the castle stands close both to a twelfth-century church and to a modern farm whose name, the Bu of Wyre, reflects the great Norse hall which preceded it demonstrates that this was the site of the family seat. All these factors make it difficult not to accept the surviving castle ruin as the

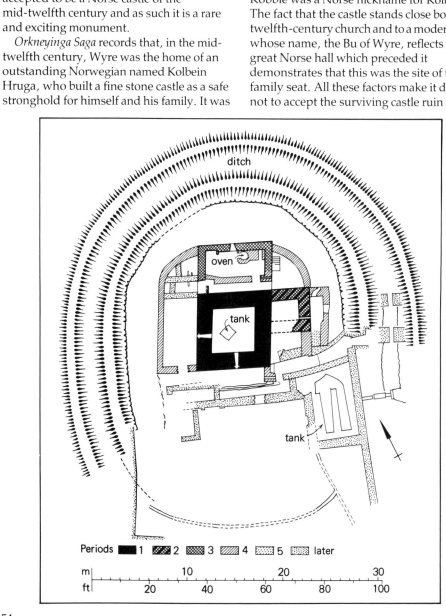

54

work of Kolbein Hruga in the mid-twelfth century.

The original building was a small stone tower set within encircling ramparts, the entire fortified area being only 23 m by 29 m in extent. The outer defences consisted of a ditch, almost 2 m deep to its flat bottom, with a low earthen rampart outside it and a strong stone wall on its inner side. The southern part of these defences has not survived for it was demolished to make room for later buildings at a time when the castle had lost its defensive character. The wall survives to a maximum height of about 1.2 m, but it is 2.2 m thick and could well have risen considerably higher in its original form. Inside the wall a second shallow ditch was dug into the natural bedrock in order to leave a central platform on which the tower was built. The entrance through all these outer

The rock-cut ditch at Cubbie Roo's castle revealed during excavations.

defences is on the east, where the outer ditch was bridged by flat stone slabs resting on piers of dry-stone masonry. There is a second pair of piers just to the north of the entrance but their function is uncertain—a drawbridge resting on the two is considered unlikely.

The tower itself is almost square and measures 7.8 m by 7.9 m overall. At its base the walls are 1.7 m thick and they survive to a height of about 2 m; only the ground floor of the tower remains, and the narrow ledge (or scarcement), which supported the joists for the first floor, can be seen on the inner face of the N wall. The surviving ground floor was probably used as a storeroom, accessible only by ladder from the first floor, because there is no doorway and the entrance into the tower must have been in the first floor above—a first-floor doorway was in fact seen and recorded in 1688. The walls are built of undressed flagstones laid in lime mortar and they rest directly on bedrock. A roughly

rectangular tank has been dug into the rock floor of the storeroom, possibly to hold an emergency water-supply. Two narrow slits open through the w and s walls, each rebated near the outer end to take a wooden window-frame. The outside of the tower was originally plastered. It is impossible to be certain how high the tower stood when first built; at least three floors would have been necessary in order to achieve a reasonably clear view over Gairsay Sound.

Much of the site was excavated in the 1930s; a fragment of medieval mail was found, but the most important result was the disentanglement of the various structures on the platform round about the tower. The site was evidently maintained in use over a long period, for at least five building-phases were identified apart from the tower itself. Additional wings were built on to the tower, first against the E wall and then on the N; the latter includes an oven built against its N wall at a later date. Subsequent buildings covered the rest of the platform round the tower and finally extended southwards over the levelled outer defences of earlier periods. It is not absolutely certain to which period the defences belong but it is possible that they and the tower together represent the original castle of the twelfth century.

Situation 1.2 km sw of the landing place on the NW side of the island of Wyre. OS 1:50,000 map sheet 6; HY 441263.

22   Orphir Church, Mainland

The remains of Scotland's only surviving circular medieval church may be seen at Orphir on the mainland of Orkney overlooking Scapa Flow. About two-thirds of the church was dismantled to provide stone for the later parish church which, until taken down recently, partially overlaid it; the line of the wall may be seen and the apse is still intact. The church consisted of a nave, 6.1 m in internal diameter within a wall about a metre thick, and an apse opening off the E side of the nave. The apse measures 2.18 m in width and length and is vaulted at a height of 3.6 m above the original floor. The curve of this half-barrel vault forms the arch between nave and apse. Light is provided by a round-arched window in the E end of the apse, and beneath the window is a seating for an altar. The nave would also have had a vaulted ceiling with a central sky-light.

The church was built in the first half of the twelfth century and was dedicated to St Nicholas. Its circular plan was derived ultimately from the Church of the Holy Sepulchre in Jerusalem; this was the period of the great Crusades, and the circular church became popular over much of Europe as the returning crusaders brought with them the idea of copying the famous church in

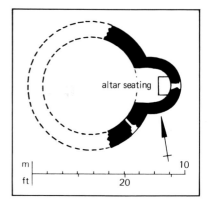

altar seating

Jerusalem. Earl Hakon Paulsson, who died in 1122, went on pilgrimage to Jerusalem and his seat in the Orkneys was at Orphir. He may well have instigated the building of what *Orkneyinga Saga* describes as a 'magnificent church'.

The same passage in the saga describes the main hall of the Earl's residence, or Bu, which stood beside the church. The remains of a large building have been excavated and are still visible near the round church but they cannot with certainty be dated to the same period.

Situation About 14.5 km sw of Kirkwall (A 964) on the shore of Scapa Flow. OS 1:50,000 map sheet 6; HY 334044.

The round church at Orphir from the air with, in the foreground, the Earl's Bu. (Reproduced by kind permission of the Royal Commission on the Ancient and Historical Monuments of Scotland)

23 St Magnus Church, Egilsay

This small and low-lying island is dominated by the unusually beautiful church of St Magnus. It consists of the normal rectangular nave and square-ended chancel and has the addition of a tall round tower at the west end, which makes the church a unique survival of a group of churches that once existed in the Northern Isles, distinguished either by a single tower or by a pair of towers.

The church is built of mortared whinstone rubble and the walls, which still stand to their full height, are plastered internally. The tower has survived to a height of 14.9 m but it is thought to have been some 4.5 m higher originally (it was partially dismantled for safety in the last century) and to have had four or five storeys; the ground floor has a window facing s, the first floor has one facing w, the second floor E and the third floor has four windows, one to each quarter of the compass. The base of the tower is 3 m in diameter internally, narrowing to 2 m towards the top. The entire building is now roofless, but an early nineteenth-century sketch shows a gabled roof of stone slabs over nave and chancel and a conical slab roof on the tower. The gables were finished with crow-steps.

Internally the nave measures 9 m long and 4.7 m wide, and there are two opposing entrances towards the w end. Both are original and, like the doorway into the ground floor of the tower, display rounded arches. There are also two original round-arched windows, together with two lintelled

57

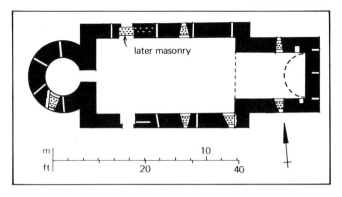

windows in the s wall which are later insertions. Entry into the chancel at the E end of the nave is through an arch formed by the continuation of the barrel-vaulted ceiling which covers the chancel, an area 4.6 m long

by 2.9 m wide. Both windows (now blocked) are original, and the purpose of the two small recesses to the E of each window is uncertain. There used to be an upper chamber above the chancel; its small lintelled window can still be seen in the E gable, and above the chancel arch is a doorway opening from this chamber into the roof space above the nave. At the

St Magnus Church, Egilsay.

same level at the w end of the nave a similar doorway led into the first floor of the tower.

The church is dedicated to St Magnus and was probably built in the mid-twelfth century—it is thought not to be the church in which Earl Magnus prayed before his murder around AD 1117. He was killed at the order of the rival Earl Hakon so that the latter might rule alone over the Orkneys. It is not known whether the existing church was built on the same spot as the earlier church.

Situation About 700 m E of the pier on the w side of the island of Egilsay. OS 1:50,000 map sheet 6; HY 466303.

24 Eynhallow Church, Eynhallow

Eynhallow is a small uninhabited island lying between Rousay and the E coast of mainland Orkney, a quiet haven for birds and seals. Its name comes from the Norse *Eyin-Helga* or Holy Isle and indicates its early importance as an ecclesiastical site. The island would appear to have had a monastic settlement in the twelfth century; *Orkneyinga Saga* relates how the foster-son of the great Kolbein Hruga of Wyre was kidnapped from Eynhallow in 1155, and it is most probable that the boy had been sent there to be educated by the monks. The only surviving building which is as early as the twelfth century is the church, which was reconstructed as a dwelling house in the sixteenth century. The existence of the early church fabric was unsuspected until 1851. The building was one of four cottages whose occupants caught a fever and were taken off the island; the roofs of the cottages were removed in order to make them uninhabitable, and, in the process, the fabric of the earlier church was discovered.

The church consisted of a rectangular nave with a porch at its w end and a square-ended chancel at the E end. Of the walling visible today, only the porch, the w and E gables of the nave and the lower part of the inner face of the chancel walls are original. The rest represents the sixteenth-century

The church on the island of Eynhallow.

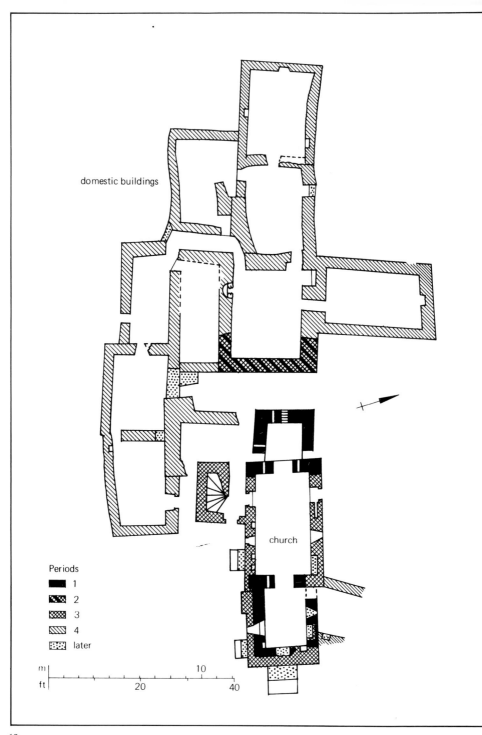

domestic buildings

church

Periods
■ 1
▨ 2
▨ 3
▨ 4
▦ later

m
ft
10
20
40

reconstruction. There are three doorways into the porch, of which those in the W and N walls are closest to their original form and are less than half a metre wide. The head of the northern doorway has a single block of stone dressed into a rounded arch with slight moulding on one side. The porch measures about 2.3 m square and opens through a rounded archway into the nave, which was originally 6.3 m long and 3.5 m wide. There is good stonework surviving at the pointed chancel arch, but the chancel itself, an area 3.8 m by 2.6 m, has been much altered by later domestic building.

Situation On the S side of the island of Eynhallow. OS 1:50,000 map sheet 6; HY 359288.

25 Pierowall Church, Westray

The Bay of Pierowall on the E coast of Westray has long been a focus of settlement. A large cemetery of pagan Viking-Age graves was discovered in the sand dunes here in the nineteenth century, and it was to this safe natural harbour that Earl Rognvald and his men came in 1136 at the start of his subjugation of the Orkneys. *Orkneyinga Saga* relates that Rognvald attended a service in the church at Pierowall; this was the predecessor to the building which still stands, but it is not known whether the earlier church was on the same spot.

The oldest fabric of the surviving church dates from the thirteenth century, but most of the visible building represents later alterations carried out in the seventeenth century—the date of 1674 is carved on the S skewput of the gable separating nave from chancel. The original church consisted of a rectangular nave approximately 14.5 m long and 5.8 m wide, with a chancel at the E end. The nave was widened by about 0.5 m in the seventeenth century, by rebuilding the W, N and E walls and retaining the old S wall to form the basal 2 m of the present S wall. At the same time the chancel was reconstructed as a 'laird's aisle', which is out of alignment with the nave by being canted southwards. Two formerly recumbent grave-slabs have been built into the wall at the E end of the church; they are good examples of seventeenth-century funerary monuments.

Situation At Pierowall, Westray. OS 1:50,000 map sheet 5; HY 439488.

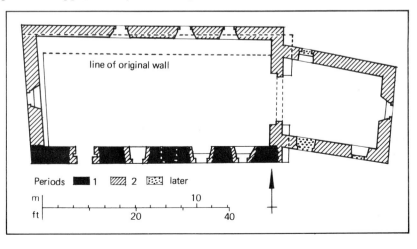

line of original wall

Periods ■ 1 ▨ 2 ▨ later

m ────── 10

ft ────── 20 ────── 40

The seventeenth-century grave-slabs in Pierowall Church,
Westray.

26 Westside Church, Westray

The present-day situation of Westside church is somewhat unexpected; it lies on the W coast of the island of Westray, very close to the sea and yet not now close to a good landing-place even though there are sandy bays on either side, but it almost certainly owes its location to the presence of an important settlement of late Norse date, which existed about 70 m to the E.

The structure visible now includes the nave and chancel of the twelfth-century church together with an extension at the W end of the nave built at some later period. The original nave was 4.2 m wide and 5.7 m long, and was later extended to a length of 14 m by removing the W wall. The original entrance is the more easterly of the two and has a rounded arch, as does the sole surviving window. The chancel is entered at the E end of the nave through a rounded arch similar to that of the original entrance but here supported on slightly inclined jambs. Inside, the square-ended chancel measures 2.8 m by about 2 m; both chancel and nave are slightly wider at the W ends than at the E. The entire church is now roofless, but traces of the original barrel-vault over the chancel can still be seen.

Westside eventually became a parish church and it may have been at this time that the nave was extended to accommodate a larger congregation. The church stands in a small burial-ground.

Situation On the S shore of the island of Westray, 5.7 km S of Pierowall. OS 1:50,000 map sheet 5; HY 455431.

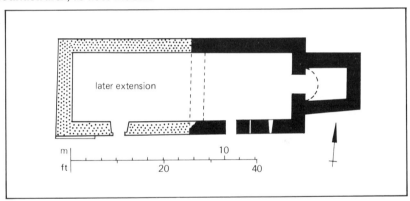

later extension

Westside Church, Westray.

27 St Mary's Chapel, Wyre

The dedication of the small church on the island of Wyre is now uncertain, possibly because it never became a parish church, and it has been attributed to both St Mary and St Peter. It was built in the late twelfth century, and it is evident that some restoration must have been carried out privately in the late nineteenth or early twentieth centuries for the fabric is today rather more complete than when a sketch was made of it in 1866.

The church consists of a rectangular nave, 5.9 m by 4 m internally, with a square-ended chancel which measures 2.4 m long and 2.2 m wide. Both the chancel arch and the entrance in the centre of the w gable of the nave have semicircular arches and are of equal width. Only one of the two original windows in the nave survives and, like the window in the s wall of the chancel, it is of lintelled form. Traces of the original plaster can be seen both in the nave and in the chancel, and the present harling on the outside of the church seems to have replaced plasterwork.

The church stands close to Cubbie Roo's

St Mary's Chapel, Wyre.

Castle and was presumably built by the same Norse family whose seat was in Wyre. *Situation* 1.2 km sw of the landing place on the NW side of the island of Wyre. OS 1:50,000 map sheet 6; HY 443262.

---

28 Bishop's Palace, Kirkwall

The town of Kirkwall is dominated by the noble cathedral of St Magnus founded by Earl Rognvald in 1137. W Douglas Simpson has vividly evoked the impact on the small community of the building of the cathedral in the twelfth century. 'Let us picture in our minds the concourse of highly skilled imported craftsmen who must have settled down among the dry-stone and turf-roofed huts of the local inhabitants. There would be the skilled masons and imagers, the carpenters and plasterers, the glaziers and the tilers and the painters, the workers in metal, the jewellers and enamellers and the makers or merchants of rich and costly vestments and altar-cloths. The advent of all these craftsmen-artists, and of the swarm of purveyors who supplied their needs, must have involved a social revolution in twelfth-century Kirkwall. And into the midst of this hive of creative, artistic activity comes the great building Bishop himself with his

court—the ordainer and deviser, under his noble patron, of the whole vast enterprise, transferring to the immediate neighbourhood of the rising cathedral his own episcopal residence from the outlying station of Birsay.' The Bishop in question was William the Old (1102-68), and it has been suggested that the earliest part of the Bishop's Palace was his episcopal residence. The Bishop's Palace and the adjacent Earl's Palace are in state care and, as a detailed guidebook to the monuments is available, only the main phases need be outlined here. The main rectangular block of the Bishop's Palace forms what is known as a hall-house, comprising a series of cellars, above which the major apartment or hall was built; only the lowest portion survives and we can only conjecture the arrangement and furnishings of the hall itself in which the Norwegian King Hakon died in 1263 after defeat at the Battle of Largs, but it may well have been a sombrely splendid residence.

In the second period of building, Bishop Reid (1541-58) reconstructed and heightened the main block and built the round tower at the NW angle. The three buttresses of the W wall appear to be a later addition. Simpson has suggested that the final reconstruction was carried out about 1600 by Earl Patrick Stewart, who made it into a detached part of his own Palace and may even have housed in it some of the fifty musketeers he is said to have retained. The visitor should try in his imagination to reinstate in the rather gaunt interior of the Palace the timber floors of the upper levels, reached by the spiral staircase in the tower, and the attendant bustle and colour of the Earl's court.

Situation In Kirkwall, S of the Cathedral. OS 1:50,000 map sheet 6; HY 449108.

Bishop's Palace, Kirkwall.

29 Earl's Palace, Kirkwall

'The Earl's Palace forms three sides of an oblong square, and has, even in its ruins, the air of an elegant yet massive structure, uniting, as was usual in the residence of feudal princes, the character of a palace and of a castle.'

Sir Walter Scott in his novel *The Pirate* describes both the architectural interest of the Earl's Palace and its atmosphere. Erected shortly after 1600 by Patrick Stewart, Earl of Orkney, this spacious residence comprises three main apartments, a great hall and two smaller rooms on first-floor level set above a series of cellars or storehouses. The Renaissance doorway has impressive but now rather worn carved details. The main hall is elegantly proportioned with a bold three-light window at the s end and a large lintelled fireplace with faceted jambs on the N wall; Scott envisaged the immense chimney as testifying to 'the ancient Northern hospitality of the Earls of Orkney'. The eclectic carved decoration throughout the building is equally remarkable, drawing on French and Elizabethan sources. The balanced SW facade with its generously fenestrated bay and oriel windows and its

Earl's Palace, Kirkwall.

provision for gun-loops is in keeping with its dual role as a palace and a castle.

Situation In Kirkwall, s of the Cathedral. OS 1:50,000 map sheet 6; HY 449107.

30 Earl's Palace, Birsay, Mainland

Overlooking the NE end of Birsay Bay are the remains of the residence of the late sixteenth-century earls of Orkney; although the Palace has become considerably dilapidated in recent centuries, the W facade still gives an impression of austere grandeur. The Palace was constructed around a courtyard with projecting rectangular towers at the corners except at the NW. The range on the N side is rather later than the main period of building. The masonry is of split blocks with lime mortar, some of the stones of the w side being particularly large, and only in the first-floor window jambs of the w exterior is freestone employed. The corner towers, the courtyard and the N range are provided with numerous gun-loops. Although the Palace courtyard is now entered from the s there was

originally also a subsidiary entrance in the centre of the w wall; this is now blocked and it is not indicated on a seventeenth-century plan of the Palace now preserved in Register House, Edinburgh. This drawing and one a century later provide some impression of the Palace in its original more open setting with gardens and plots to the E; they also show the elegant s facade with the central doorway, with the initials of Robert, Earl of Orkney, above the lintel, and the date of 1574 over a window above it. If the drawing is correct, the decorated window pediments of the E and N elevations would have provided a welcome enrichment to the exterior of this sombre building; five pediment finials were recovered in 1929 from the well in the centre of the courtyard. The Palace is still in the course of conservation and, although it is possible that further features of architectural interest may be found, it is difficult for the visitor to imagine the 'sumptuous and stately building' as it was described in 1633. The rooms on the upper storey were decorated and in the late seventeenth century the ceilings were said to be painted with biblical subjects such as the Flood and the Entry into Jerusalem with the appropriate text given beside the illustration.

Situation Near the shore at Birsay at the NW of Mainland and at the end of the public road (A 966). OS 1:50,000 map sheet 6; HY 248277.

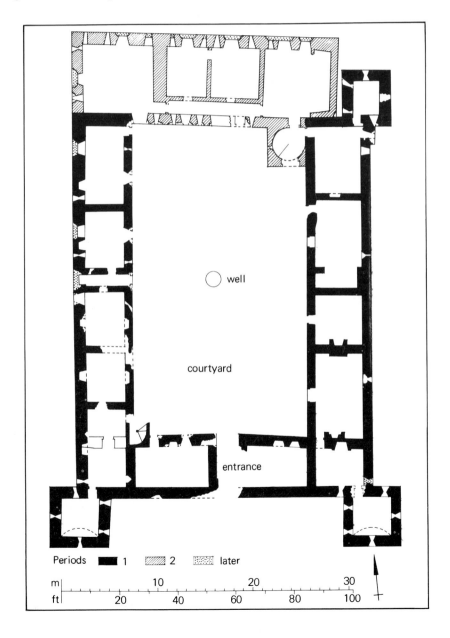

well

courtyard

entrance

Periods ■ 1 ▨ 2 ▨ later

m ┤————— 10 ————— 20 ————— 30
ft ┤——20—— 40 —— 60 —— 80 —— 100

An eighteenth-century drawing of the Earl's Palace, Birsay.
(Reproduced by kind permission of Edinburgh University
Library)

31 Noltland Castle, Westray

Noltland Castle is an austere and formidable stronghold standing 1 km W of Pierowall; details of its history and architecture are described in an individual guide-leaflet. Begun in 1560, it is an excellent example of a

Noltland Castle, Westray. The entrance is covered by many gun-loops. In the foreground is the courtyard.

Z-plan castle, comprising towers at diagonally opposite corners of a main block; this allowed for increased accommodation and possibly greater privacy than did the simple tower-house, but it also had important defensive advantages for the use of firearms. At Noltland, the almost extravagant provision of gun-loops provides a telling character assessment of the builder, Gilbert Balfour. The approach to the doorway is through a courtyard of later date than the castle and the entrance in the sw tower is well-covered by gun-loops. The main features of interest to the architectural historian are the plan, the gun-loops and the main spiral staircase, the newel of which is surmounted by a richly carved capital; there is an extensive view from the eastern battlements.

Situation 800 m w of Pierowall on the island of Westray. OS 1:50,000 map sheet 5; HY 429487.

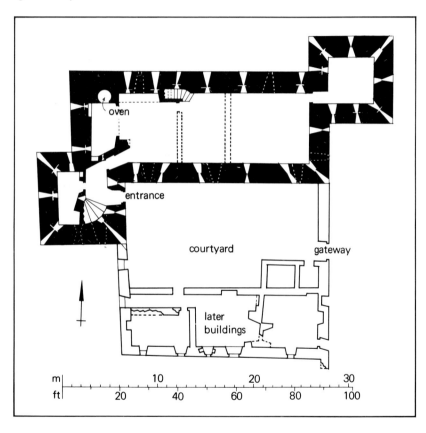

32 Click Mill, Dounby, Mainland

Water-mills were never as numerous in the Orkneys as they were in Shetland, where natural water-power is far greater, but a fine example has been preserved in working order near Dounby. It represents the most primitive type of water-mill recorded in Britain, which is known as the 'horizontal mill' or, more popularly, as the click mill or clack mill from the sound that it makes when running. The characteristic feature of these mills is that the wheel is set horizontally instead of vertically and their design is simply a mechanized version of the old hand-quern. The type seems to have been developed first in the Middle East, and it is thought that it may have been introduced into Scotland by Irish missionaries in whose homeland the horizontal mill had been in use since the early centuries of the Christian era. This particular mill was built in the early nineteenth century and it follows the same pattern as earlier mills.

Situation 3.5 km NE of Dounby (B 9057). OS 1:50,000 map sheet 6; HY 325228.

Click Mill, Dounby. The machinery is all still in working order.

33 Martello Tower, Hackness, Hoy

The impressive Martello Towers, built to guard the deepwater inlet of Longhope between North Walls and South Walls at the SE end of the island of Hoy, are testimony not to the defence of Orkney against Napoleonic invaders, as is so often assumed, but against the navy and privateers of the United States of America. The United States declared war on Britain in June 1812 as a result of British harassment of American vessels trading with Napoleon's allies; American successes in western and northern waters and particularly in threatening the Baltic trade made the assembly place for convoys especially vulnerable. Vessels met in the Sound of Longhope and then, under the protection of a warship, crossed the North Sea. Artillery defence of the anchorage was provided between 1813 and 1815 by the construction of a battery and tower at Hackness on the S side and by a tower at Crockness on the N; the former tower is in state care; restoration work is not yet complete and only the outside may be viewed.

The function of the tower was to provide a firm foundation for a 24-pounder cannon and living quarters for NCO and gunners. The ground plan of the tower is elliptical, for the seaward wall is twice as thick as that facing inland to provide additional protection against bombardment. The internal arrangements are circular with the cannon carriage on the open upper storey; the living area has cubicles for the gunners and is lit by two windows; the only door into the tower is at a height of about 4 m above ground level outside. The ground floor contains various stores and the all-important magazine; the stairs leading to these floors are situated within the thickness of the seaward wall. The towers were renovated in 1866 and were used in the First World War. Like the Churchill Barriers of later times, the Martello Towers are a reminder of the strategic naval importance, and indeed vulnerability, of the Northern Isles.

Situation At Hackness, in the SE of Hoy, on the NE tip of the peninsula of South Walls. OS 1:50,000 map sheet 7; ND 338912.

Hackness Martello Tower on the island of Hoy.

	Name of Monument	Location	Opening Hours
1	Unstan Chambered Tomb	Stenness	†Standard
2	Blackhammer Chambered Tomb	Rousay	All times
3	Knowe of Yarso Chambered Tomb	Rousay	All times
4	Midhowe Chambered Tomb	Rousay	All times
5	Taversoe Tuick Chambered Tomb	Rousay	All times
6	Maes Howe Chambered Tomb	Stenness	Standard
7	Cuween Hill Chambered Tomb	S of Finstown	†Standard
8	Wideford Hill Chambered Tomb	W of Kirkwall	All times
9	Quoyness Chambered Tomb	Sanday	†Standard
10	Holm of Papa Westray Chambered Tomb	Holm of Papa Westray	All times
11	Dwarfie Stane	Hoy	All times
12	Knap of Howar	Papa Westray	All times
13	Skara Brae	Sandwick	Standard
14	Stones of Stenness	Stenness	All times
15	Ring of Brodgar	Stenness	All times
16	Gurness Broch	Evie	Standard
17	Midhowe Broch	Rousay	All times
18	Grain Earth-house	Kirkwall	†Standard
19	Rennibister Earth-house	Firth	All times
20	Brough of Birsay, Church and Viking Settlement	Birsay	Standard
21	Cubbie Roo's Castle	Wyre	All times
22	Orphir, Earl's Bu and Church	Orphir	All times
23	St Magnus Church, Egilsay	Egilsay	All times
24	Eynhallow Church	Eynhallow	All times
25	Pierowall Church	Westray	All times
26	Westside Church	Westray	All times
27	St Mary's Chapel	Wyre	All times
28-9	Bishop's and Earl's Palaces	Kirkwall	Standard
30	Earl's Palace, Birsay	Birsay	All times
31	Noltland Castle	Westray	†Standard
32	Click Mill	Dounby	All times
33	Martello Tower*, Hackness	Hoy	All times

* Can be viewed only from the outside.
† Keykeeper monuments.

Notes

Standard Hours
April to September—
Weekdays 9 30 am to 7 pm   Sundays 2 pm to 7 pm

October to March—
Weekdays 9 30 am to 4 pm   Sundays 2 pm to 4 pm

Monuments on Mainland are easily accessible. The Brough of Birsay is on a tidal island. Crossing is impossible during the period approximately three hours before High Water to three hours after. High Water is one hour before High Water Kirkwall, which is posted at the Harbourmaster's office there. There are no crossings by boat and in winter the monument is closed on Mondays.

The intending visitor to monuments on the islands of Egilsay, Eynhallow, Rousay, Holm of Papa Westray and Wyre is advised to contact the local Tourist Office to arrange beforehand for motor-boat transport.

Visitors to Sanday, Westray, and Papa Westray should consult the steamer or air-service time-table. Steamers leave from Kirkwall.

The intending visitor to Knap of Howar on Papa Westray should contact the local Tourist Officer to arrange beforehand for motor transport.

Printed in Scotland for HMSO by McQueen Printers Ltd., Galashiels.
Dd. 762149 C85 4/86